THE D-DAY
ASSAULT

THE D-DAY ASSAULT

A GUIDE TO THE NORMANDY LANDINGS
AFTER 70 YEARS

Stephen T. Powers
Kevin Dennehy

GTCI Press
Denver, Colorado

Published by GTCI Press
Cover by Bright Sun Creative

ISBN-13: 978-0615972961

We dedicate this book to our parents,

Mary Tallichet Powers and John Nathaniel Powers,

and

Deirdre Edna Dennehy and Daniel John Dennehy.

Normandy veterans at Utah Beach on June 6, 2014

TABLE OF CONTENTS

INTRODUCTION

We have had it happen to us probably more than once. You are driving along on a vacation trip and suddenly you spy a sign indicating that you are passing an old battlefield or military museum. You wonder if you should stop--wondering if it is worth the delay. Should you have known something about the site before you left home? To this day, you still don't know.

This is where we hope our second edition guidebook, *The D-Day Assault, A Guide to the Normandy Landings after 70 Years*, will prove invaluable to the military history traveler to the holy grail of World War II sites--the Normandy landing beaches. Our goal is to be able to provide current information about battlefields, military museums and even military cemeteries. The inherent problem with published guidebooks, and there are many good ones for the sites we cover, is not only are they expensive to publish and purchase, but they become obsolete and out of date quickly. Road nets change, new monuments and memorials are dedicated, older monuments are moved to new location, museums change their displays and hours of operation, to say nothing of their admission prices.

The Normandy battlefields we visit are a perfect example. In the past few years, several new museums, memorials, monuments and exhibits have opened. However, others have closed. The road from Caen to Bayeux to Cherbourg, N 13, was rebuilt into a modern divided-lane highway, and access to the American and German cemeteries have been radically changed. And more change is inevitable.

Because of these ever changing conditions, we have chosen to publish this guidebook and its associated website, www.dday70th.com, in an effort to keep you informed with the most current information as possible. We think we can provide you with a more comprehensive view of the experiences a traveler is likely to encounter. One first tip: do not leave established footpaths, particularly at Omaha Beach, the grass is slippery and you can fall.

This new edition contains 20 more pages than our original guidebook, with new photos, museum entries and other updated information.

We understand that you will probably not be travelling alone, and that your family or companions may not share your enthusiasm for military history, so we also intend to include information not found in the usual battlefield guide--information on local sites of interest, lodging, dining, non-military museums where they exist and book and movie reviews.

We look for your contributions and critical input on our website, as well as Amazon.com as we go forward. We also hope you have a pleasant and informative trip as you visit the Normandy landing beaches.

Stephen T. Powers and Kevin Dennehy
Denver, Colorado
April 2015

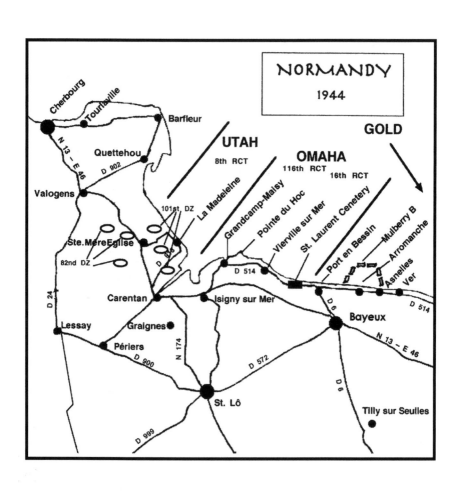

OMAHA AND UTAH BEACHES AMERICAN DROP ZONES

TOUR

In more than 70 years since the end of World War II, the Normandy battlefield has become sacred ground to Allied soldiers of that era in the way that the Gettysburg, Antietam, Verdun and Somme battlefields did for their earlier counterparts. Today, hundreds of monuments, plaques, and memorials dot the Norman landscape. And there will be more to come. It is as if the WWII generation is saying to the rest of us that "here we stood, here we made our statement, our sacrifice for human freedom." It is a battlefield more honored, more revered by Americans, than any of the hundreds of other WWII battlefields, with the possible exception of the Arizona Memorial at Pearl Harbor.

It is impossible, of course, in the space we have here to take you to every one of these sites to explain the meaning and significance of the monuments and memorials that stand there. The best we can hope to do is guide you to some of the more significant. In "The D-Day Assault" we will concentrate on the landing beaches, American, British and Canadian, along with the parachute drop-zones.

GETTING THERE

We assume that if you have not arranged for a guided tour of the Normandy beaches, you have access to a car. Probably the simplest course to take would be to rent a car in Paris and drive to Bayeux on A 13-E 5, the *Autoroute de Normandie*. It is not as intimidating as you may think. Once you find the Paris *périphérique*, it's only a matter of time before you reach the exit to the *Autoroute*, but, be sure you enter the *Autoroute* going the correct direction, which is indicated by the name of the *Port* (exit) toward which you are heading. It is about 240 kilometers from Paris to Bayeux, with numerous rest stops along the way.

If you don't have a navigation system with a European map database, be sure to acquire the most recent Michelin maps of France (#989) and of Normandy (#231).

En route to Normandy should be a stop at the Memorial Center for History and Peace in Caen. Don't let the name fool you. This museum is one of the finest military museums in the world. Opened just before the 50th anniversary of D-Day, the museum exhibits take you through an engrossing tour of the events leading to the 1939-45 war in Europe and the war itself, focusing on D-Day and its aftermath. The museum tour ends with a film that makes an eloquent plea for world peace. Exhibits make use of artifacts, photographs, ship models and the latest A/V technology to tell this compelling story.

If you can possibly arrange it, take the elevator down to the water garden to spend a few minutes contemplating what you have just seen. Memorial houses a book store/souvenir-shop, a library-documentation center and restaurants on the main floor.

If you decide not to drive, guided tours of the beaches can be arranged through the Memorial Museum (see the museum section for contact information) and through Holts Tours: Battlefield & History Tours in England. Phone (International): 00 44 843 178 3701; (UK) 0843 178 3701 or through their web site: info@holts.co.uk. Leger Holidays, a UK leader in battlefield tours, recently acquired Holts. There are several other companies that provide guided tours. Check the Trip Advisor web site for information and reviews. It is actually possible to rent a jeep in Caen, with or without a guide. Contact Lerat in Caen. Phone: +33(0)2.31.75.22.15; Fax: +33(0)2.31.75.25.85.

If you are up for a long lunch break on the drive down from Paris, you might leave the A-13 *Autoroute* at the Vernon exit (exit 16) to visit Claude Monet's country home at Giverny, located just outside the village. Drive through Vernon and across the Seine, and then immediately pick up D 5 southeast to Giverny. Although Giverny is not a WWII site, it is a short drive and well worth the detour, especially in the summer when the gardens are in full bloom. Expect a crowd. Also, be sure to browse through the gift shop inside the Monet compound and those in the village. You might also consider visiting the new Musée des Impressionismes and the town of La Roche-Guyon, farther along D 5, where Field-Marshal Rommel maintained his headquarters in the local château.

GUIDES AND ROUTES

It has become commonplace to break this complex, extensive battlefield into discrete itineraries for the purpose of guiding the visitor around the area. Tonie and Valmai Holt's "Battlefield Guide to the Normandy Landing Beaches" (1999) splits the battlefield into five itineraries. "The March to Victory" (1986; 1994) by John T. Bookman and Stephen T. Powers does it in three. The informative, free pamphlet "The D-Day Landings and the Battle of Normandy" (2001), published by the Calvados, Manche, and Orne tourist departments describes eight tours. The routes designated by the tourist offices are now signed with a post carrying a stylized, silhouetted bird, the name of the route and important information about the site. The routes we suggest you take correspond roughly to the one marked, "D-Day-Le Choc" (shock or onslaught).

Look for this sign along the way –

Keep in mind that the smaller "D" roads in Normandy can be quite narrow and winding. Drive and park accordingly.

There are also 10 distinctive monuments, likened to a ship's prow, erected by the Comité du Débarquement (hereafter CD monuments) years ago that mark important sites on the Normandy beaches. The work of the Comité, along with that of the Coastal Conservation Trust in acquiring important sites, makes the Normandy battlefield one of the best preserved and best marked of all World War II sites.

The places that we consider essential for you to visit while exploring the Omaha and Utah Beach areas are:

- *Mémorial, Musée pour la Paix* in Caen.

- Bayeux (the Musée Mémorial de la Bataille de Normandie and the British Commonwealth Cemetery and Memorial).

- The American Cemetery at St. Laurent-sur-Mer.

- The Vierville (D-1) Draw area.

- The Pointe du Hoc.

- The Winters and Easy Company Memorials.

- La Madeleine.

- Ste.-Mère-Église.

Give *Mémorial* a half-day and Bayeux a full day. The tour outside of Bayeux can be completed in another full day. That means that you will need three days to do justice to the American beaches and landing zones alone.

MÉMORIAL

The museum is located off the northern half of the Caen ring road (N 814 that becomes N 13—A 46 as you leave Caen). The turnoff is well signed and parking is ample near the museum. See our section on museums for further details.

BAYEUX

Since we are advising travelers to stay in Bayeux, it seems appropriate to begin the battlefield tours there.

Bayeux was liberated on D-Day +1 by elements of the 50th British Infantry Division, a fact attested to by a plaque across from the south side of the cathedral. Bayeux was fortunate in that it was neither bombed nor fought over during the invasion, thus it escaped the destruction visited upon other Norman towns such as Caen, Falaise and St.-Lô.

Bayeux and Vicinity

As you enter the city, you can't help but notice the imposing bronze statute of Gen. Dwight D. Eisenhower standing before a triumphal arch where the N 13 divides. It is an exact copy of the statue that has long stood in Grosvenor Square in London.

You may want to visit the Musée Mémorial du Géneral de Gaulle (10 rue Bourbesneur), housed in the old Governor's mansion in the center of Bayeux, where you can find mementos of his visit to Bayeux on June 14, 1944. There is also a plaque commemorating his visit and the speech he gave in the nearby Place Charles De Gaulle, two blocks east of the cathedral. Two sites off the Boulevard Fabian Ware are well worth visiting – the Musée Mémorial de la Bataille de Normandie and the British Commonwealth Cemetery and Memorial.

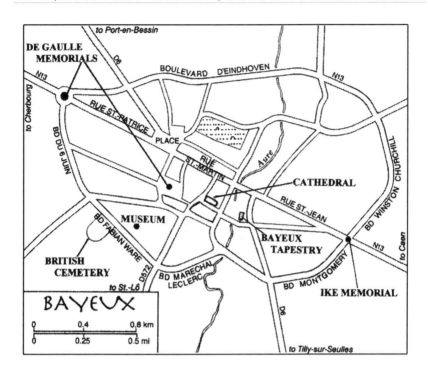

Accommodations in Bayeux

Before we talk about the American participation in the 1944 Normandy invasion of continental Europe, let's digress for a moment to talk about accommodations in the area.

The most advantageous base from which to visit the American beaches and drop zones is the city of Bayeux, with the much larger Caen a second possibility. Most likely by the time you read this it will be too late to make reservations at most Bayeux hotels for the 71st Anniversary of D-Day. Even if you are not visiting the landing beaches at that time, it is wise to make reservations as far in advance as you are able — two years at least.

In Bayeux, four hotels stand out: the three star Le Lion d'Or with its excellent restaurant (71 rue St.-Jean; Phone: +33(0)2.31.92 06.90), the Hôtel D'Argouges, housed in a small 18th century chateau, (21 rue St.-Patrice; Phone:

+33(0)2.31.92.88.86), the newer, more expensive, Churchill, opened in 1986 (14 rue St.-Jean; Phone: +33(0)2.31.21.32.80) and the very highly rated and expensive Villa Lara (6, Place du Quebec; Phone: +33(0)2.31.92.00.55). These hotels are all centrally located and within walking distance of Bayeux restaurants and historical sites.

Both Ibis and Novotel operate less expensive hotels on the outskirts of town.

These hotels and others can be booked with online services: www.tripadvisor.com, www.expedia.com and www.orbitz.com. The TripAdvisor site also offeres evaluations by recent visitors that may provide some help in your choice of accomodations.

If you are camping, we can recommend the Château de Martragny, a member of "Les Castels" chain (Ph: +33(0)9.72.50.09.13 for reservations; Web: www.les-Castels.com), located off N 13, near the village of Martragny, 8 km east of Bayeux. The spacious camping areas surround an 18th century chateau that serves as a residence for the owners. Le Château de Martragny is open May to 15 September. Ph: +33(0)2.31.80.21.40;   Fx:+33(0)2.31.08.14.91;email: chateau.martragny@wanadoo.fr.

There are several campgrounds near Utah Beach as well. Once again, the TripAdvisor web site is useful in booking accommodations.

Dining

If you stay at the Lion d'Or, a full restaurant is available in-house; the other hotels have only breakfast service. There are also several restaurants facing the Place St.-Patrice, numerous small sidewalk cafes along the rue St.-Jean (Le Drakkar, 27 rue St.-Jean, is typical), and some fast food places off rue St.-Martin.

All are easily accessible by foot from any of the hotels that are centrally located.

The TripAdvisor website now rates 73 Bayeux restaurants, with La Rapiere at 57 Rue St.-Jean currently holding down the number one spot.

In season, the moules marinière are excellent in Normandy. If you are adventurous, try the Tripe à la Caen, a regional specialty, and don't forget to order some Camembert or Pont-l'Evêque for your after dinner cheese course with a snifter of Calvados, the local apple brandy.

Regional specialties you won't want to miss:

Camembert and Pont l'Evèque. Local aged Camembert made from unpasteurized milk is soft and pungent – the full monty. You either love it or hate it. Pont l'Evèque is its milder, nutty cousin. Ste.-Mère-Èglise produces its own *Petit Ste.- Mère-Èglise.* Try some after you visit the Airborne Museum.

Calvados and Cidre. Calvados, the local apple brandy, gives up little or nothing to its more famous cousins from the Cognac region to the south. The cider is much less alcoholic and a delight to drink.

Tripe a là Caen. Like Camembert, the local tripe dish is not for the faint of heart. Some local Bayeux restaurants have it as a menu staple.

Moules marinière. While steamed mussels are not unique to Normandy, the local variety are simply wonderful. Norman restaurants also specialize in a variety of seafood dishes.

Shopping

Small shops are scattered throughout the central part of the city. There is a supermarché along the Boulevard D'Eindhoven and a hypermarché off N 13, halfway between Bayeux and Caen.

The gift shop in Memorial sells a wealth of D-Day mementos and souvenirs at reasonable prices, as do the gift shops in other D-Day museums.

Things to see and do in or near Bayeux

Besides the sites associated with the D-Day beaches, and related monuments and memorials, Bayeux offers the traveler a number of interesting attractions:

- **Bayeux Tapestry.**

- **Cathédrale Notre-Dame.** The Cathedral, dominating the center of the city, is classic French Gothic dating from the 12th Century. It contains some interesting stained glass and both WWI and WWII memorials.

- **Saturday market in the Place St.-Patrice.** This market is one of the great open-air markets in Europe. Booths contain everything from fruits and vegetables to local cheeses and handcrafts to live chickens and ducks. In 2002, two locals were selling paella out of a three-foot pan. Make sure you have a free Saturday morning in Bayeux so you won't miss it.

- **Other street markets.** In the summer, vendors have set up booths along the Rue St.-Jean that offer an amazing variety of local products. St. Lô and Carentan also hold markets on Saturday mornings.

- **Musèe Baron Gèrard.** A ticket to this museum is included with the one to the Centre Culturel (Bayeux Tapestry). The museum, located on the Place des Tribuneaux, has displays of ceramics, local lace and porcelain, and paintings and furniture from the 16th through 19th centuries. Open daily 9-7 June-August; hours are shortened during the remainder of the year.

Tapestry and Embroidery

Bayeux Tapestry: World's first propaganda poster?

The Bayeux Tapestry: This artistic masterpiece commemorates the Normand conquest of England in 1066. Today, it is housed in a permanent gallery in the Bishop's Palace in Bayeux and is open to the public. The self-guided tour consists of a short sound and light show setting the stage for the invasion of England by William, Duke of Normandy and subsequent Battle of Hastings, followed by a walk-by of a facsimile of the tapestry. The facsimile panels are accompanied by plaques that explain their meaning. This walk is followed by a viewing of the Tapestry itself, which is displayed in a long Plexiglas-protected, horseshoe-shaped case (the Tapestry is actually a scroll 225 feet long and just under 20 inches wide) under subdued lighting. The entire tour takes an hour or more or, if time is pressing, the

Tapestry itself can be viewed in half that time. Expect crowds in the summer. Centre Culturel, rue de Nesmond. Open daily, 9-7 from June through September. Opening times vary from October to May. Admission charge.

The Overlord Embroidery: Across the Channel, housed in the D-Day Museum in Portsmouth, England, is the Bayeux Tapestry's modern counterpart, the Overlord Embroidery. Commissioned in 1968 by Lord Dulverton, the Embroidery was designed by Miss Sandra Lawrence and produced by the Royal School of Needlework. In a series of thirty-four panels (272 feet in total length), it depicts the events leading up to and including the 1944 invasion of Normandy. Many of the panels were taken from photographs, thus include historic personages as well as more abstract scenes. Open daily from April to October (except 24-26 December), 10-5:30 (5:00 in winter). Admission charge. Phone: (023) 9282 7261; Fax: (023) 9287 6550; E-mail: info@ddaymuseum.co.uk; www.ddaymuseum.co.uk

Probably, the most direct way to reach Omaha Beach from Bayeux is to take the Boulevard D'Eindhoven as it swings north around the city until you reach the D 6 exit. From there it is only 9 km to Port-en-Bessin, roughly the dividing line between Gold and Omaha Beaches.

Just before you reach Port-en-Bessin, you will pass the Musée des Epaves du Débarquement, a museum displaying equipment and other items relating to the landings recovered from the sea.

If you like, drive down into the port along the long estuary, after first negotiating the roundabout named after Gen. De Gaulle.

PORT-EN-BESSIN

Port-en-Bessin is today an active fishing port with a number of seafood restaurants scattered around the waterfront area. On D-Day+1, the 47th Royal Marine Commando, commanded by Lt. Col. C. F. Phillips captured the port after a hard fight. A CD monument on the outer mole commemorates that assault, as does a plaque on a German blockhouse near the waterfront.

A sign, as you enter the town, proclaims Port-en-Bessin to be the "First Oil Terminal of Liberty" because of the fuel landed here before the first of the PLUTO (Pipe Line Under The Ocean) installations were in operation.

OMAHA BEACH

AMERICAN MILITARY CEMETERY AND MEMORIAL

You will now have to back track back to D 514, the two-lane road that runs back from and parallel to the coastline. Driving west will soon take you by Colville-sur-Mer, where you will pick up the signs to the Normandy American Military Cemetery and Memorial. Turn down the drive leading to the cemetery and park in the large lot on its east side. Be sure to lock your car and take valuables, such as purses and cameras, with you. Car break-ins are not unusual near the Normandy historic sites.

A new 30,000 square foot Visitor's Center opened in May 2007. You should go through the Center before touring the Cemetery itself for a better understanding of your visit. The Center is open daily from 1 April to 15 September 0900-1800 and from 0900-1700 the remainder of the year.

From the parking lot you can either enter the cemetery itself or walk directly toward the bluffs to see the remains of the German WN-62 strong point, a monument honoring the units of the 5th Engineer Special Brigade and an obelisk commemorating the men of the 1st Infantry Division who were killed on D-Day and in the weeks that followed.

Spirit of American Youth

The cemetery itself can be entered through a side gate from the parking area, now marked by a NTL signpost to indicate a stop on the French Department of Tourism's "D-Day-Le Choc" route. This signpost announces:

The American Cemetery at Colleville – The Longest Night.

Visitor,

Look how many of them there were

Look how young they were

They died for your freedom

Hold back your tears and be silent.

Today, the most striking American presence in Normandy are the 9,386 Carrara marble crosses and Stars of David that stand row on row in the American Cemetery. It is only fitting that your tour of the American sectors of the Normandy beachhead begins here.

The remains of Americans killed during the invasion and the fighting in its aftermath were re-interred here after the French Republic had ceded the 172.5 acres to the United States. They had previously been buried in three nearby locations – the present site of La Cambe German Military Cemetery, along the beach between Les Moulins and Vierville and near Ste.-Mère-Église – each marked today by a plaque. The cemetery, formally opened on 18 July 1956, is laid out in the form of a Latin cross with a chapel located at the intersection of the arms. A reflecting pool connects the chapel with an arc of colonnaded loggias featuring maps and narratives of the subsequent campaigns in Northwestern Europe. In the center of the arc stands a bronze nude figure representing the "Spirit of American Youth Rising from the Waves." A wall of remembrance, inscribed with the names of 1,557 individuals whose bodies were never recovered, completes the loggia area.

Three soldiers awarded the Medal of Honor are buried here: Brig. Gen. Theodore Roosevelt, Tech. Sgt. Frank Peregory and 1st Lt. Jimmie W. Monteith. Their crosses are further marked with a gold star and the inscription "Medal of Honor."

Thirty-nine pairs of brothers also rest here, as well as a father and son, Col. Ollie Reed and Ollie Reed, Jr.

Well inside the cemetery grounds you will find an information center and comfort area. Here also, staff can help you with locating a particular gravesite and answer questions relating to the cemetery. Also, look for the time capsule that is to be opened on June 6, 2044.

The cemetery is now more famous than ever because it was used in the opening and closing scenes of Steven Spielberg's 1998 film "Saving Private Ryan."

Obvious paths lead you to the seaward side of the cemetery where an overlook commands an excellent view of Omaha Beach. The colorful orientation table near the iron railing will enable you to locate yourself in relation to the various Beach sectors, each given an phonetic and color code designation.

Directly beneath you is Easy Red Sector defended by four German strongpoints (Wiederstandnester 66-69; abbreviated hereafter as WN-xx), where Companies E and F, 2nd Battalion, 16th Regimental Combat Team (1st Infantry Division) were to have landed in the first wave just after 0630. According to the detailed landing plan, they were to have been preceded by Company B of the 741st Tank Battalion (amphibious DD tanks), followed by the remainder of the reinforced RCT and, some three hours later, by lead elements of the 18th Regimental Combat Team (the assault configuration of the 18th Infantry Regiment, 1st ID).

But chaos reigned on the beach below. Because of high waves and a long run to the beach only four DD tanks made it ashore, whereupon one was immediately knocked out by German fire. Likewise, only one boat section from each company made it ashore, losing much of their equipment in the deep water. The remaining landing craft were swept by the tidal current and nasty weather further east to Fox Green, where the losses in both men and equipment were horrific. Four boat sections from Company E, 116th Infantry, also came ashore on Fox Green and were promptly shot to pieces, taking thirty casualties within minutes of landing, including company commander Capt. Laurence A. Madill.

Musée D Day Omaha at Vierville-sur-Mer — beach fortification

Here and there other boats sections came ashore with light casualties – two from the 116th RCT (29th ID) on Fox Green, more than a mile east from their designated landing spot. Further east on Fox Red, Company L of the 16th RCT made it to the shingle relatively intact and ready to fight its way up the bluffs.

By 0800, the situation on Omaha Beach was critical. Very little of the close fire-support had materialized from the DD tanks and from tanks ferried to the beach in LCTs. During the morning U.S. Navy destroyers had moved inshore to fire directly at German strong points. At this close range, the flat-trajectory 5-inch naval guns proved effective. Slowly, and largely due to the efforts of a few hundred American GIs, the tide of battle was turned. Gen. Bradley contemplated ordering the follow-up waves to land over the British beaches. Fortunately for the Allied cause, he did not because GIs in small groups had managed to cross the beach from their shelter along the shingle bank and climb the bluffs, now on fire and hidden in smoke, from where they were able to suppress fire from the German positions. By midday, it was becoming clear that the landings on Omaha Beach were not going to be defeated at the high water mark.

If you continue down along the path, you will reach another orientation table that describes the artificial harbor built to supply the American beachheads. Mulberry A, as it was known, was destroyed in the great storm of 19-21 June. Salvaged pieces of the Mulberry were moved to the British Mulberry at Arromanche; other pieces can be seen off Vierville-sur-Mer. As it turned out, the Mulberries were not critical for the supply effort. The U.S. Navy was able to "dry out" its LSTs — ground them at high tide so they could be unloaded directly onto the beach and then float them off again on the following high tide.

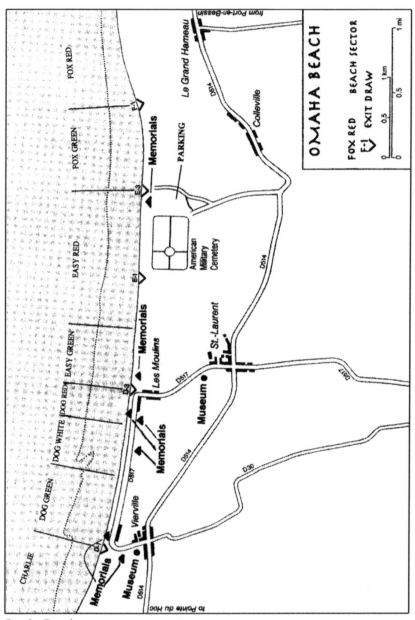

Omaha Beach

VIERVILLE: DOG AND CHARLIE SECTORS

On leaving the cemetery, take note of the two new museums that are only a short distance from the cemetery entrance — the Big Red One Assault Museum and the Overlord Museum, both of which are listed in our museum section.

From the roundabout leading into the cemetery turn west on D 514 and drive to the village of St.-Laurent. In St.-Laurent, turn on D 517 toward the beach. Here you will pass a small museum – OMAHA. Ahead of you is one of the large CD monuments that commemorates the landings on Omaha Beach, this one bearing inscriptions to the 1st and 29th IDs. If you turn east along the beach road, note the memorials to the 2nd ID and the Provisional Engineers Special Brigade (and the PESB's bunker). Now heading west, note the plaque commemorating Operation AQUATINT, a failed 1942 British commando raid. Further down the road is a stele marking a temporary cemetery where American dead were first buried.

The beach road that you are driving parallels the Dog Red, Dog White and Dog Green sectors of Omaha Beach where the 116th RCT (a Virginia National Guard unit, whose antecedent was the famous Confederate Stonewall Brigade) landed.

At Vierville, where the road turns away from the water, there is a cluster of memorials and the narrative of what happened there explains why.

Here, the National Guard Association has seen fit to place a memorial to all the National Guardsmen who fought in France in both World Wars. It sits atop a former German bunker. A small stone, commemorating the 58th Armored Field Artillery Battalion, stands nearby.

The wreckage of the American artificial port, Mulberry A, can be best seen from this vantage point.

There are two stone memorials in the median of D 30 (the road leaving the beach area) – one dedicated to the 29th ID that lists the Division's WWII campaigns, battle honors, and battle casualties (some 19,814 men killed, wounded or missing in action); the other, moved from its original location and rededicated in 1998, commemorates the men of the 6th Engineer Special Brigade. A memorial, dedicated to the Rangers of the 5th Ranger Battalion who died here, stands on the west side of the road way. Next you will pass the D.Day OMAHA museum, a convenient place to pause and contemplate D Day events here.

National Guard Monument, Omaha Beach

The events on these three beach sectors were as traumatic as the scenes already described on the Easy and Fox sectors further east. The assault on Dog Green was carried out by three units – Company B of the 743rd Tank Battalion in sixteen DD tanks, six boat sections of LCAs from Company A, 116th RCT, followed by a command boat, and three LCMs (Landing Craft, Medium) carrying units of the 146th Special Engineer Task Force. Their collective story exemplifies much of what went wrong on Omaha Beach.

Interpretive Sign at Omaha

The tankers of Company B were the first to come under German fire. Because of the rough weather, the DD tanks could not be launched off shore. As the LCTs carrying them attempted to beach, one was sunk by German fire. The eight surviving Shermans gave what fire support they could to the troops landing behind them.

29th Infantry Division Monument dedicated on June 6, 2014

The men of Company A were already taking heavy losses. LCA 5 foundered a thousand yards off shore, drowning six soldiers. Boat 3 was hit a hundred yards out, killing thirteen. No one saw Boat 6 sink; there were no survivors and only half the bodies were recovered. The remaining three boats grounded on an offshore sand bar. As the heavily laden infantrymen staggered off the boat ramps, they were hit by machine-gun fire. Something like half the men from Boats 1 and 4 died in the water within a few feet of the ramps, some from gunfire, and others by drowning. All the surviving officers and sergeants were wounded. Those men still alive allowed the incoming tide to carry them to the beach, where they attempted to take shelter behind beach obstacles, many to be hit there. Within minutes of landing, Company A no longer existed as a fighting unit; within half an hour, two-thirds of the GIs were casualties.

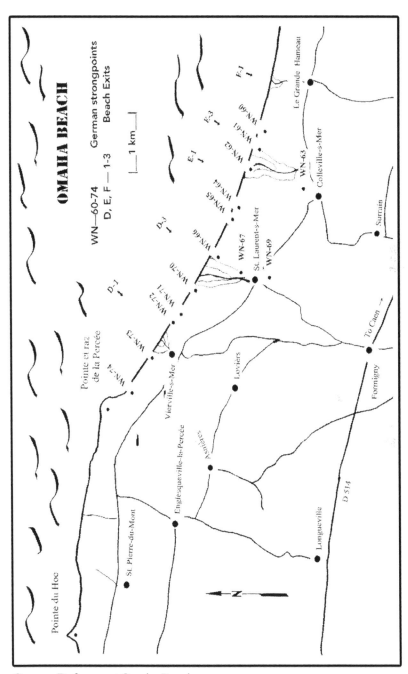

German Defenses at Omaha Beach

Further to the west, on Charlie sector, two boat sections of Company C, 2nd Ranger Battalion, landing at 0645, were also under heavy fire. One of the LCAs was hit, killing the company commander and a dozen men. Fifteen more Rangers were hit exiting the second boat. By the time the survivors reached the bluffs, over half the Ranger force were casualties. This was the landing that inspired the opening combat scenes in the film "Saving Private Ryan."

Some boat sections coming in on Dog White, Dog Red and Easy Green sectors made it ashore relatively unscathed; others suffered fates similar to companies A and C. At 0730, the Command Group made it to the beach on Dog White, where Brig. Gen. Norman D. "Dutch" Cota, the 29th IDs second in command, and Col. Charles D. W. Canham, commanding the 116th RCT, took charge. At their urging, men from the 5th Ranger Battalion and Company C blew gaps through the beach wire and seawall, made it across the 150 yards to the bluffs and, covered by smoke from the grass fire now burning, worked their way to the top. Cota personally led one group of GIs up, and then returned to the beach to rally the men there. By 0830, the GIs had suppressed German fire from the crest. Both Cota and Canham won Distinguished Service Crosses for their efforts, and Cota actions on the beach are enshrined in the 1962 film "The Longest Day," in which he was portrayed by actor Robert Mitchum.

Gen. Bradley, who had only imagined the carnage and wreckage on Omaha Beach that morning from the deck of the cruiser *Augusta*, would later write that "every man who set foot on Omaha Beach that day was a hero." It's not hard to see why. You may think that the opening scene from "Saving Private Ryan" was a bit overdone; it wasn't. Casualties on Omaha Beach that day numbered some two thousand, roughly half of whom were killed. By contrast, the Marines took fifteen hundred casualties landing on Tarawa Atoll a little over six months before, and that was considered a major disaster. To put these losses in perspective, remember that the Army of the Potomac lost 12,000 men in one day at Antietam 82 years earlier and that the Allied air forces had lost 2,000 planes and 12,000 airmen in the previous two months.

POINTE DU HOC

Continue west along D 514 toward the small port of Grandcamp-Maisy. First you will pass the Château d'Englesqueville, the grounds of which housed the 147th Engineer Combat Battalion in June 1944. The stone with plaque is on private land, but the owner, M. Lebrec, welcomes visitors.

In a little over 8 km you will see signs directing you to the Pointe du Hoc, the D-Day objective for companies D, E and F of the 2nd Ranger Battalion, commanded by Col. James E. Rudder, a reserve officer, former football coach and graduate of Texas A & M University.

The Pointe du Hoc battlefield has been improved in recent years with a new parking lot and restroom facilities, and, we might add, fresh barbed wire to keep the over-inquisitive from the more dangerous areas. Recent renovations are now complete and the site is fully open.

What strikes one immediately on seeing this battlefield is that it still looks like one. The sites that you have hitherto visited give little clue to the violence that transpired there 70-plus years ago. Not so the Pointe du Hoc. The promontory and its gun emplacements were bombed and shelled incessantly before the landings. Even though time has softened the craters and ruined gun emplacements, today you can still imagine the violence of the air and naval attack.

Ranger Monument at Pointe du Hoc is now open.

ARMY RANGERS

The U.S. Ranger Force, organized in the early summer of 1942, was the brainchild of Brig. Gen. Lucian K. Truscott, Jr. Truscott, then stationed in Northern Ireland, wanted to organize an American unit patterned on the already famous British Commandos, battalion sized units designed as quick strike forces. Truscott chose the name "Rangers," a name with historical American antecedents, to differentiate the American units from the British. The job of  organizing the new Ranger battalion fell to Maj. Gen. Russell P. Hartle, commanding American ground forces in Northern Ireland. Returning from church one Sunday, Hartle turned to his aid-de-camp, artillery Captain William O. Darby, a West Point graduate turned artilleryman, and asked if he would like to command the new unit. Darby jumped at the chance. In the short run, it was a smart career move for he was immediately promoted to major and made lieutenant colonel a month and a half later. Darby soon recruited his Ranger battalion to its authorized strength of just under 500 men, had them trained by British Commandos, and led them into action in North Africa as a component of Operation Torch. Success in North Africa prompted an expansion of the Ranger Force to three battalions, the 1st, 3rd and 4th. But, the Ranger saga came to an unhappy end in 1943 when a good part of the Force was destroyed in a German ambush outside of Cisterna, Italy. The surviving Rangers were melded with the 1st Special Service Force, an American-Canadian Special Forces outfit. After duty in the U.S., Col. Darby was assigned to 10th Mountain Division as its Assistant Commander, only to be killed by shrapnel a few days before the war ended in Italy. He was posthumously promoted to Brigadier General, the only American officer in WWII to be granted that honor.

Meanwhile, two other Ranger Battalions had been organized in England, the 2nd and 5th. These were the units that participated in the D-Day landings and fought their way across Europe in its aftermath. The 6th Ranger Battalion fought in the Philippines.

NORMANDY MEDAL OF HONOR AWARDS

These eight men were awarded the Congressional Medal of Honor for their actions in the Normandy campaign:

Cpl. John D. Kelly (Co. E, 314th Infantry, 79th Division) persisted in his attack with pole charges against an enemy pillbox on the approach to the Fort du Roule, outside Cherbourg, taking it with his third attempt. Kelly was killed on Nov. 23, 1944.

Lt. Carlos C. Ogden was commanding Company K of the 314th Infantry, 79th Division when he found his company pinned down before the Fort du Rule. Armed with an M-1 and various grenades, Ogden advanced alone under fire. Although hit in the head by a machine gun bullet, Ogden managed to take out both an 88-mm gun and a machine gun with his grenades. Ogden ended the war as a Major.

Brig. Gen. Theodore Roosevelt, Jr., Assistant Divisional Commander of the 4th Infantry Division and son of the twenty-sixth president, after submitting four requests, was allowed to land with the first wave on Utah Beach. For a large part of D-Day, Roosevelt remained exposed under enemy fire while rallying the men around him, directing and personally leading them against the enemy. Roosevelt died of a heart attack on July 12 and is buried next to his brother Quentin, a World War I casualty, in the St. Laurent cemetery.

Pfc. Charles N. Deglopper was a glider infantryman with the 325th Glider Infantry, 82nd Airborne Division. In fighting at the la Fière bridge over the Merderet River on June 9, Deglopper courageously covered his buddies while they attempted to withdraw. Even after he was wounded he continued to advance toward the German position, firing his BAR until he was killed. He was later found surrounded by dead Germans.

Lt. Col. Robert G. Cole commanded the 3rd Battalion, 502nd PIR, 101st Airborne Division in Normandy. His battalion was pinned down by enemy fire when he stood, drew his .45 and led a successful bayonet charge near Carentan on June 11. He was the first soldier in the 101st Airborne to win the Medal of Honor. Col. Cole was killed on Sept. 18, 1944, and buried in the Netherlands American cemetery.

Sgt. Frank Peregory, 3rd Battalion, 116th Infantry has been honored by the National Guard Association for his heroic actions near Grandcamp when he attacked a machine gun position with grenades and bayonet. Peregory knocked out the gun, killed eight of the enemy and captured another 35 in so doing. He was killed on June 14 and is buried in the St. Laurent cemetery.

1st Lt. Jimmie W. Monteith, Jr. (16th Infantry, 1st Infantry Division) was awarded his Medal for his actions on Omaha Beach. Landing with the first waves, Monteith remained exposed to enemy fire while urging his men to advance. After heroic efforts, he was surrounded and killed. He is buried in the St. Laurent cemetery.

Staff Sgt. Walter Ehlers. Ehlers, the last living D-Day Medal of Honor winner, died in March 2014. He was a platoon leader in the 18th Infantry, 1st ID who landed in the second wave on Omaha Beach. His squad fought its way off of the beach, and, by 9 June, were several miles inland where Ehlers destroyed several machine gun nests near Goville. The next day, he covered the withdrawal of his platoon—and carried a wounded rifleman to safety—despite his own wounds. His brother, Roland, also with the 1st Infantry Division, was killed on Omaha Beach on D-Day.

Cross marking the grave of 1st Lt. Jimmy Monteith

CEMETERIES: A REMINDERS OF THE FALLEN IN NORMANDY

IN ALL ARMIES

The concept of a military cemetery, a place where soldiers killed in battle might be buried, and thus honored and remembered, only dates back to the middle of the 19th century. The British Empire in the Crimean War and the United States in the Civil War were the first modern nations embrace the concept.

As the United States entered World War I, the War Department promised to repatriate the remains of the doughboys killed abroad if requested by the immediate family. All others were to be buried in cemeteries located near battlefields where they died. The permanent grave sites were to be marked by either Latin Crosses or Stars of David, each inscribed with name, rank, unit, state of birth and date of death. Medal of Honor winners and high-ranking officers had their inscriptions picked out in gold. Where an individual gravesite was not possible, the names of the deceased were to be inscribed on a wall of remembrance. The eight American cemeteries created after World War I resemble large, grassy parks dotted with an occasional tree, a serene place where one might take a picnic lunch if it were allowed.

After World War II, the American Battle Monuments Commission added another 14 cemeteries that are scattered from Europe to Alaska to Hawaii. Because of the repatriation policy, less than 40 percent of American World War II dead still remain abroad; some 172,000 have been brought home. Today, the Army's Casualty and Memorial Affairs Operations Center still seeks to identify and reclaim American military dead from all wars.

Both the British Commonwealth and the Federal Republic of Germany, through the Commonwealth War Graves Commission and the Volksbund Deutsche Kriegsgraeberfuersorge, maintain cemeteries in Normandy, as do the French and Polish governments through their respective agencies. In Normandy alone, there are two American, five German, one French, one Polish and 19 British Commonwealth cemeteries. Other gravesites may be found scattered in village churchyards. With certain time restrictions, all these cemeteries are open to the public.

POINTE DU HOC (continued)

If you stand at the top of the 100-foot cliff today, you can almost, but not quite, see the beach where the three companies landed on D-Day morning because of barbed wire strung to prevent visitors from approaching too close to the cliff's edge. The sheerness of the cliff from any vantage point still remains impressive.

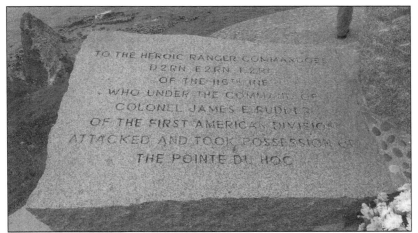

Monument to Rudder's Rangers at Pointe du Hoc

In the early dawn and rough weather, Rudder's little flotilla had made for the wrong landfall, the Pointe de la Percée, instead of its intended objective, the Pointe du Hoc, three miles farther west. Rudder discovered the navigational error before it was too late and turned his boats to the west, but, as they bobbed along parallel to the coastline, they were swimming ducks for the Germans along the bluffs. And, they were 40 minutes late. The last bombing raid was long over. An LCA, a DUKW amphibious truck and a supply boat sank on the run in to the narrow beach on the east side of the Pointe. The Rangers fired rocket-propelled grappling hooks as they landed, but many failed to hang up in the wire along the cliff top. Nevertheless, in the face of stiff German resistance, with the grappling ropes available and climbing sectional steel ladders, the Rangers scaled the cliff and drove the defenders from their trenches. (DUKWs [amphibious-trucks] carrying long fire ladders were useless because they couldn't clamber up the shingle.) Much to Rudder's surprise, the casemates were devoid of guns. Only later in the day did patrols pushing inland find the six 155-mm howitzers and spike them. Mission finally accomplished.

German position overlooking Pointe du Hoc

But, the Ranger position on the Pointe was precarious. Rudder had not been able to contact the remainder of the 2nd Battalion or the 5th Ranger Battalion, both waiting offshore to reinforce his landing. As a consequence, both units landed on Charlie and Dog Green to the east and wouldn't reach Rudder's position for two days. The Ranger force was thus left exposed to German counterattacks; casualties began to mount. Rudder was eventually able to get a signal out to V Corps with a Navy signal lamp, "Located Pointe du Hoe, mission accomplished – need ammunition and reinforcement – many casualties."

Fortunately, HMS *Talybont* and USS *Satterlee*, a prewar Buchanan class destroyer with two of her newer consorts, *Barton* and *Thompson*, moved inshore to provide fire support for the Rangers. The *Satterlee* alone fired 638 rounds of 5-inch ammunition that day, which was about average for the more than 20 American destroyers supporting the landings.

When finally relieved two days later, Rudder's command had been reduced from some 200 to around 90 effectives.

German Blockhouse on Pointe du Hoc

The Ranger Memorial on the Pointe du Hoc, standing on a former German blockhouse at the tip of the point, is a dramatic, knife-like spire of granite flanked by tablets inscribed in French and English.

Continue west on D 514. In about 4 km you will pass a monument and memorial garden dedicated to the memory of Sgt. Frank Peregory, 3rd Battalion, 116th Infantry, who is buried in the American Cemetery and was awarded the Medal of Honor for his actions on 8 June. This memorial was dedicated in 1994, as part of the 50th anniversary celebration.

A small museum, dedicated to retelling the Ranger epic, is located on the Quai Crampon in Grandcamp (see our section on museums for further information). A NTL signpost, detailing Grandcamp's role as an Allied port, stands in front of the museum.

An impressive memorial to two French squadrons (Guyenne and Tunisie) that flew missions with the British Bomber Command stands near the quay's northeast corner. The French units participated in the bombing of German gun emplacements near Maisy. The memorial was dedicated with great fanfare in 1988.

The tour of Omaha Beach sites ends at this point. It is possible to continue through Isigny and Carentan to Utah Beach, and then on to Ste.-Mère-Église and/or Cherbourg.

ISIGNY, BRÉVANDS AND CARENTAN

Leave the Grandcamp-Maisy area by D 514. New highway construction now bypasses the old N 13 route, but if you chose to detour into Isigny and Carentan you will find the effort rewarding.

Isigny dedicated a stained glass window in its church (1 rue Victor Hugo) in 1994 commemorating the 29th Division, which liberated the ruined town on 8 June. Before you reach the church you will pass a CD monument and a NTL signpost expounding Isigny's place in the invasion scheme.

The village of Brévands, on D 444 between Isigny and Carentan, also has installed a commemorative window in its church. Brévands is where GIs first met on 10 June to complete the linkup between Omaha and Utah Beaches. To see the window, you will have to make a half hour detour from N 13.

The Normandy Tank Museum recently opened off old N-13 just east of Carentan. For more detail on its location, see our entry in the Museums Appendix.

Leave N 13-E 46-E 3 at the roundabout complex just short of Carentan and pick up D 974 (Voie de le Liberté) that will take you into the town and beyond.

The CD monument and NTL signpost stand in front of the *mairie* (town hall) in Carentan. The 101st Airborne Association dedicated a commemorative plaque at the site in 1973. The city also sponsors a summer flower display in honor of the 82nd AD. Inside the *mairie* you will find various flags and other mementos.

Leave Carentan on N 974 headed toward St.-Côme-du-Mont. Stop by the 502nd PIR memorial in front of an Agralco warehouse.

During the night of June 11, the 3rd Battalion of the 502nd had just managed to cross the last of the four rivers blocking the road to Carentan when it was pinned down by German fire. Lt. Col. Robert Cole, commanding the battalion, here led a bayonet charge across what was then a cabbage patch that cleared the way into the town. Cole received the Medal of Honor for his actions; another of his officers, Maj. John Stopka, was awarded the Distinguished Service Cross. Neither officer survived the war.

Continue on D 974 through the northwestern outskirts of Carentan and stop at the Cole memorial.

On June 4, 2014, a U.S. military contingent along with French civilians dedicated this memorial stele, located about a kilometer short of Dead Man's Corner, that commemorates Lt. Col. Cole's bayonet charge. It is very close to the 1944 cabbage patch where the charge took place. There is limited parking at this site.

Another small museum, the Dead Man's Corner Museum, occupies an old house between Carentan and St-Côme-du-Mont at the junction of D 913 and D 974 about a kilometer past the Cole Memorial. See our entry in the Museums Appendix.

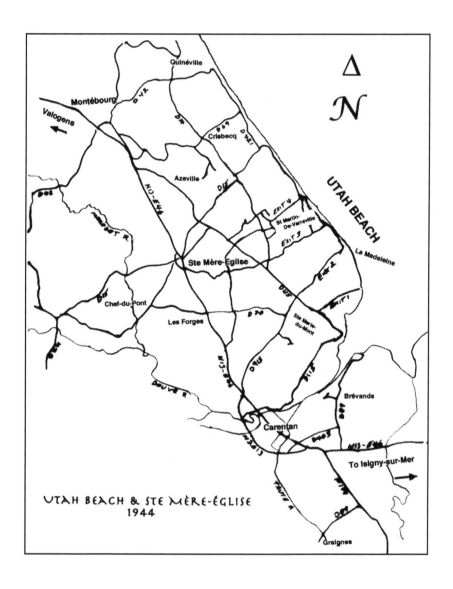

UTAH BEACH & STE MÈRE-ÉGLISE
1944

UTAH BEACH AND BEYOND

At Dead Man's Corner, D 974 joins D 913, a road that will take you to Vierville, Ste.-Marie-du-Mont and La Madeleine. Utah Beach is about 14 kilometers distant and is today crowded with memorials and monuments, with surely more to come.

Approximately one kilometer before reaching Ste.-Marie-du-Mont, turn east (a sign marks the turn) to find a stone commemorating the A 16 airfield used by the 36th Fighter Group, Ninth Air Force. The 36th flew P-47s in close support of ground troops and was awarded two Distinguished Unit Citations for its efforts.

While driving through Ste.-Marie-du-Mont notice 14 signs (in French) posted around the village describing D-Day events there.

Lt. Dick Winters, Easy Company and the action at Brécourt Manor.

On the road north from Ste.-Marie-du-Mont (D 913) you will pass a memorial to Lt. Richard D. Winters erected by the WW II Foundation, a non-profit based in Kingston, RI. The monument, an imposing 12 feet in height, was dedicated on June 6, 2012 with some surviving member of Easy Company, 506th PI, 101st Airborne Division in attendance. The memorial is capped by a realistic statue of Winters, shown running with a M-1 Garrand in one hand, urging his men forward. The base is inscribed with the words "dedicated to all those who led the way on D-Day" in both English and French. It also carries a quote from Winters himself —"Wars do not make men great, but they do bring out the greatness in good men." The WWII Foundation commissioned this memorial from Alabama sculptor Stephen Spears, who also has sculpted several other monuments on Utah Beach.

Dick Winters first came to the attention of those interested in the history of the 1944-45 campaign after Stephen Ambrose published an account of Easy Company, 506th PI in "Band of Brothers" (New York, 1992), making Winters a central character. The story of Winters taking a small group of men from Easy Company into their first combat on June 6 at nearby Brécourt Manor is well chronicled by Ambrose and realistically recreated by Steven Spielberg and Tom Hanks in their partially-fictionalized mini-series adaptation, "Band of Brothers" (2001). We highly recommend that you read "Band of Brothers" and view the mini-series. Even so, we will attempt here to recreate the Brécourt Manor action and give you directions to the Manor. In the night drop during the early hours of D-Day, Easy Company was badly scattered (as were most of the parachute units). Dick Winters came down just outside Ste.-Mère-Église with only his bayonet stuck in a boot. He quickly found other members of Easy Company, rearmed himself and began to move north toward Ste.-Marie-du-Mont. Soon, Winters made contact with members of the 2nd Battalion staff and was ordered forward to deal with a previously undetected battery of four 105-mm howitzers, connected by a trench system, which had just opened fire on Utah Beach from a position near Brécourt Manor. Given orders to attack the German position, Winters assembled a small group of paratroopers (12), a number from Easy Company, and advanced toward the German battery after positioning machine guns on his flanks. Winters' men assaulted the German position in three groups using their rifles, Thompsons and grenades to attack Germans in the trenches and gun emplacements. In the confused fighting that followed, Winters and his men succeeded in over-running the German positions and spiking the four cannon; the attackers lost four dead and two wounded while killing 15 Germans gunners and paratroopers and capturing 12 more out of a enemy force of about 50.

Lt. Winters' superior officers nominated him for the Congressional Medal of Honor for his heroic action, but he received the Distinguished Service Cross instead.

Richard Winters' Memorial near Ste.-Marie-du-Mont

(Only one Medal of Honor was allotted to each Division; the Screaming Eagle's medal went to Lt. Col. Robert G. Cole, commander of the 3rd Battalion, 502nd PIR, who led the bayonet charge near Carentan on June 11). All of the other members of Winters' squad received lesser medals. Winters survived the war and realized his dream of settling down in rural Pennsylvania where he died in January 2011.

Brécourt Manor is most easily reached from Ste.-Marie-du-Mont by exiting the Place de l'Église via the Rue des Mannevilles (D 424) to the northwest. You will pass The Musée du Debarquement d'Utah Beach on your left. Drive 1 km and then turn right (north) onto Brécourt Drive. Continue north for .5 km until you pass the Manor (a large farm complex) on your right. The attack described above took place in the fields on your left (west), however the earthen gun emplacements and trenches are no longer visible.

A small memorial has been placed near the Manor that commemorates Easy Company and its fight nearby. Look for the American and French flags flying over the memorial that mark its location.

Three kilometers north of Ste.-Marie-du-Mont on D 913 you will pass the imposing statue of a merchant seaman, placed here by the Danish government to commemorate the 800 Danish seamen who served aboard Allied merchant ships.

LA MADELEINE

Pause as you reach this beach area because the landings on Utah Beach took place right in front of you. The imposing white, Utah Beach museum is built over German blockhouse WN5. The pre-invasion bombardment put WN-5 out of commission and wounded its commander, Lt. Arthur Jahnke, before he could launch his GOLIATHS — small, remote controlled tanks filled with explosives — largely neutralizing the German defences along this sector of Utah Beach.

The Neptune plan called for the landing of 32 DD tanks directly ahead of the 2nd Battalion of the 8th RAT, 4th ID a kilometer or so to the northwest in front of causeway 3. Five minutes later they were to be followed by the 1st Battalion along with naval demolition teams and combat engineers. Other units were to follow in quick succession. None of this happened as planned. Tidal currents swept the first wave a kilometer to the south, playing havoc with the precise landing timetable. Coming ashore with the first boats, the Assistant Divisional Commander, Brig. Gen. Theodore Roosevelt, Jr., made the decision to land the succeeding waves on the new beach, uttering (or maybe not) the famous words, "We'll start the war from right here." In any case, Roosevelt was awarded the Congressional Medal of Honor for his efforts that morning. But, the Medal was awarded posthumously, for he died of a heart attack a month later. There were four roads or causeways that led inland across marshy ground behind Utah Beach. The landing force was tasked to capture their seaward ends, while the airborne troops were to secure the landward sides. La Madeleine lies at the seaward end of causeway #2, essentially the road over which you have just driven, so this quickly became the preferred beach exit instead of #3 further north. Teams of combat engineers and naval demolition units immediately set out to blow gaps in the seawall and wire, and clear mines for the GIs landing now in ever increasing numbers. All the while, they were being harassed by incoming small arms and 88-mm fire. At Roosevelt's and his regimental commander's urging, they cleared the obstructions while taking minimal casualties. Naval vessels offshore covered the landing with gunfire all day. In his memoirs, Omar Bradley called Utah Beach "a piece of cake." That might have been an exaggeration, but compared to the landings on Omaha Beach, it almost was.

The ubiquitous Sherman with the older 75-mm cannon.

Many memorials and monuments stand in the area around La Madeleine, but the principal attraction is the Musée du Débarquement, first opened in 1962 and now refurbished and enlarged. Adjacent to the museum squats an M4E8 Sherman tank, an amphibious tractor, an American 90-mm antiaircraft gun and an American LCVP (Higgins boat). Nearby are memorials to many of the units and individuals who played a role in the D-Day landing or were landed over Utah Beach later. Among them are:

- An obelisk commemorating the 4th U.S. Infantry Division, the division that stormed ashore here on D-Day.

- A NTL signpost.

- The first of the 1,182 cylindrical milestones (this one is designated 00) marking the beginning of the *Voie de la Liberté,* the route of the U.S. Third Army from Normandy to Bastogne. All are decorated with 48 stars and a symbolic torch of liberty patterned after the one held aloft by "Liberty" in New York harbor. The markers mimic the stones that line *La Voie Sacrée*, the road from Bar-le-Duc to Verdun along which so many thousands of French soldiers advanced in 1916, never to return.

- An imposing, 24 foot-tall, red-granite obelisk, dedicated by Maj. Gen. J. Lawton Collins, VII Corps Commander, at the 40th Anniversary celebration to commemorate the VII Corps that Collins commanded so ably. It stands "in humble tribute to its sons who lost their lives in the liberation of these beaches, June 6, 1944." The American Battle Monuments Commission maintains the site.

- Another 40th Anniversary plaque commemorating the then contemporary Allied leaders who attended that ceremony — U.S. President Ronald Reagan, Queen Beatrix of the Netherlands, Prime Minister Pierre Trudeau of Canada, Queen Elizabeth II of Great Britain, King Baudouin of the Belgians, King Olaf of Norway, Grand Duke Jean of Luxembourg and French President Pierre Mitterrand, all now fading into history as well.

- A stone marker to commemorate the 90th U.S. Infantry Division, units of which were attached to the 4th ID for the assault on D-Day, and that landed over Utah Beach in the days that immediately followed. The 90th was a reactivated World War I National Army Division recruited originally from the states of Texas and Oklahoma, hence the T/O divisional patch. Calling themselves the "tough 'ombres," the 90th had a tough time in Normandy, but fought on to become one of the Third Army's crack infantry divisions.

- A stone commemoration Gen. Dwight D. Eisenhower as Supreme Allied Commander.

- A road sign, "Rowe Road," one of the 59 signs near Utah Beach marking roads named after men of the 1st Engineer Special Brigade who died in the fighting on Utah Beach. This sign honors Pvt. J. T. Rowe of the 531st Engineer Shore Regiment.

- A memorial to the 1st Engineer Special Brigade, dedicated in 1945, on a blockhouse of the WN-5 defensive position. The blockhouse was captured on D-Day and used as the Brigade HQ. It consists of a memorial crypt (protected by a locked grill) and several commemorative plaques. A photograph of Maj. Gen. Eugene Mead Caffy, who commanded the Brigade, is displayed in the protected part of the crypt. The Coast Guard Combat Veterans Association has also placed a plaque here dedicated to the "members of the United States Coast Guard who participated in the initial invasion of Normandy on D-Day, especially those who gave their lives here. . . ." There is an informative orientation table on the seaward side of the memorial locating, among other things, the positions the ships in Force U.

- A plaque recalling the work of the U.S. Naval Amphibious Forces on the bunker where they set up their headquarters on 8 June and remained until 31 October 1944. The names of the 41 sailors involved are listed.

- The U.S. World War II Wall of Liberty Foundation once had plans to build a memorial wall across from the museum. As proposed, the "wall" would have consisted of a series of upright tablets inscribed with the 2,900 names of those who died in the landings and the more than 77,600 American military personnel who entered France across Utah Beach. This project has been undertaken by veterans of the 29th Division because of the failure of a similar project planned for the 50th anniversary. This earlier proposed wall, for which a considerable amount of money was raised by the now defunct Battle of Normandy Foundation, was to have been built at Caen's Mémorial Museum before the project was cancelled. The WWII Wall of Liberty Foundation's plan, as of 2010, has been placed on indefinite hold because of opposition from local officials. See the Foundation's website at: www.usww2wolf.org/.

- About 250 yards to the east of the bunker complex you will find a memorial to the men of the U.S. Naval Reserve.

- And just land ward of the parade of monuments stands the bar-brassiere "Le Roosevelt" occupying a house that formally disguised a German bunker (and, actually, still does). By all means stop in to enjoy a coffee or beer and examine the display of WWII communication equipment, photographs and other souvenirs.

The WXYZ AFFAIR

Historian Stephen E. Ambrose wrote in his "D-Day, June 6 1944: The Climatic Battle of World War II" that you would not believe this story if it had not been witnessed by ten GIs. Believe it or not, Staff Sgt. Harrison Summers, 1st Battalion, 502nd PIR hailed from West Virginia, not Hollywood, yet his D-Day odyssey reminds you more of the exploits of the fictional John Rambo (Sylvester Stallone) in "First Blood," one of Hollywood's gifts to the action-hero genera.

Sgt. Summers found himself with a group of troopers at the inland side of the #4 causeway. The ranking officer present, Lt. Col. Patrick Cassidy, sent Summers with 15 men to capture a German coastal-artillery barracks located in a cluster of stone farm buildings about a kilometer or so inland and designated WXYZ. When Summers and his pickup squad reached the barracks there was a decided reluctance on the part of the rank and file to attack the buildings, but he convinced Sgt. Leland Baker to cover his flank, and then took on the complex alone.

Summers broke down the door of the first building and sprayed the room with his Thompson sub-machine gun. Leaving four dead behind him, he pursued the survivors into the next building. Pvt. William Burt, taking cover in a nearby ditch, then decided to provide some cover for Summers with his light machine gun. The intrepid sergeant next charged the third building while under fire, kicked in yet another door, then shot an additional six of the enemy. Before pursuing the survivors he was joined by a captain from the 101st AD and was able to replenish his ammo supply. But, before he could resume his attack, the captain was killed. Nevertheless, he charged the next building, leaving six more dead behind. At this point, he was joined by Pvt. John Camien, and the three men, Summers, Burt and Camien, cleaned out the remainder of the buildings. In the mess hall they caught fifteen artillerymen at lunch and shot them all. Burt's machine gun managed to set ablaze a haystack and ammunition storage shed next to the last building, whereupon 80 or so of the German defenders ran into a nearby field where some 50 were shot down. Later Summers was asked how he felt. Dragging on his cigarette, he replied that he didn't "feel very good. It was all kind of crazy."

If you drive southwest from St. Martin-de-Varreville on D 423, and cross D 14, in about .5 km you will pass a group of farm buildings (mostly to your right) that were assaulted by Sgt. Summers on D-Day morning.

Beyond Utah Beach

By continuing north on D 421, you can reach several places of interest.

Just after leaving the Utah Beach area take the first left and stop at the T-junction. The Chapelle de la Madeleine has beautiful stained glass windows and houses a photograph of GIs exiting it in June 1944.

Landing Craft (LCVP) at Utah

Continue along the beach road to reach the CD monument and a NTL signpost commemorating the landing here in July of the 2nd French Armored Division, commanded by Gen. Jacques-Philippe Leclerc, a pseudonym assumed by the Vicomte Jacques-Philippe de Hautecloque to protect his family. This Free French unit, armed and trained by the U.S. Army, although a little late arriving on the battlefield, fought with verve in the ensuing campaign and, at Gen. De Gaulle insistence, participated in the liberation of Paris and Nazi occupied France. Elements of what were later to become Gen. George S. Patton's famous Third Army also disembarked here. Today, an American M-3 personnel carrier and a M-8 armored car flank the memorials.

It was here that the leading RCT of the 4th ID was to have landed. D 423 that leads away from the beach is causeway #3. If you wander around the area, you can find remains of the fortifications comprising WN-101.

Continue on north for 4.5 until you reach Ravenoville-Plage. Here you have a choice. You can continue north on D 421 to visit the German fortifications in the St. Marcouf-Crisbecq-Azeville areas or turn east here to pick up the D 15, which will take you to Ste.-Mère-Église, 7 km away. The battery is well marked and the detour is well worth the time.

Ste. Marcouf-Crisbecq and Azeville Batteries

To reach these German batteries, continue north on D 421 for 3 km to les Gougins, and then turn east on D 69. Crisbecq and its formidable battery will come up in about 2 km. Stop by the NTL signpost.

Despite having some 600 tons of bombs dropped on it before the landings, the four 210-mm guns in this battery survived to fire on Allied ships off shore, sinking a destroyer and hitting several ships. Counter-battery fire silenced Crisbecq's guns, but the complex did not surrender until June 12, when GIs from the 39th IR captured it. This was the one German battery that actually factored in the assault on Utah Beach.

German defences at Ste. Marcouf-Crisbecq

Today, one of the bunkers houses a small museum and information center. There is a good view back toward Utah Beach and the Isles du Ste. Marcouf from its top, if you care to make the climb.

To visit the Batterie d'Azeville, continue east to D 14. Cross this road and continue on D 69, signed "Batterie d'Azeville." Turn left at the first junction onto D 269, and then take the next right (about 2 km). The casemates are across from the parking lot.

The *Wehrmacht* troops manning this complex managed to hold out for during two days. Only when Pvt. Ralph G. Riley of the 22nd Infantry used his flame-thrower to ignite ammunition inside on of the bunkers did the battery surrender. Riley was awarded the Silver Star for his courageous, single-handed attack. The casemates are open daily June-August and Sundays in May and September.

From Azeville it is a short drive east to D 115; drive southeast on that road until it intersects with D 15 at Baudiénville. Ste.-Mère-Église is 3 km away. Look for the Norman cathedral's steeple as you enter Ste.-Mère-Église and park in the lot to its south.

Ste.-Mère-Église

This small Norman town is famous today because it lay at the epicenter of the drop zones for the 82nd and 101st Airborne Divisions during the early hours of D-Day. Events in and around Ste.-Mère-Église do much to explain the difficulties facing American paratroopers during and after their night-drop.

The first wave of the American airborne assault was to be carried out by paratroopers jumping in sticks of 16 from some 816 C-47s. Another 100 aircraft towing gliders accompanied them. In all, 13,450 Americans (including six generals) landed in the Cotentin in the early hours of June 6. The results were mixed.   Only one regiment, the 505th, landed on or near its assigned drop zone.   Cloud cover and antiaircraft fire had played havoc with the tight V formations of nine planes, still losses in the air had been relatively low, between 2 and 3 percent, but as dawn broke over the Cotentin, the effectiveness of the night drop remained unknown to both the Allied and German commands.

AIRBORNE OPERATIONS

It somewhat hard to remember 70 years later how new the idea of airborne assault was in the 1940s.   The Russians, followed by the Germans, British and Americans, experimented with the idea in the late 1930s and early 1940s, but their efforts were crude and problematic.   The German 7th parachute division staged the first airborne assault of the war when it descended on Crete in May 1941.   It was not until August 15, 1942, eight months after the United States entered the war, that the U.S. Army re-designated the 82nd Infantry Division as the 82nd Airborne Division, and then quickly split it to form the cadre around which to build the 101st Airborne Division.   In 1943, the 82nd AD was deployed to North Africa and air-assaulted the Gela area of Sicily on July 9.   One of its regiments, the 504th Parachute Infantry (PIR), was subsequently dropped into the Salerno beachhead in September.   None of these operations had been particularly successful, and combat losses in Sicily had been high.   About the best that can be said is that the airborne operations had caused some confusion in the minds of the German high command.   When the 504th and the 509th PIRs were later deployed at Anzio, they were landed by sea.   After being withdrawn from Anzio, the 504tth PIR was reunited with the other parts of the 82nd AD in England.   There, joined by the unblooded 101st, the paratroopers began training for the assault on Normandy.

The night drop of the two American airborne divisions was mostly in flux in the weeks before D-Day because of German troop movements. Only at the last minute were the two divisions assigned the jobs of cutting N 13 near Ste.-Mère-Église and capturing the landward ends of the four causeways leading from Utah Beach. So uncertain were the Allied commanders about the use of their airborne forces that Air Vice Marshal Trafford Leigh-Mallory, Eisenhower's air forces C-in-C, warned of a slaughter if they were used. Ike agonized over the airborne assault, and then went ahead with the planned drop. The results were not as disastrous as Leigh-Mallory predicted (he later apologized to Ike for increasing his command burden), nor as good as the divisional commanders, Gens. Matthew B. Ridgway and Maxwell D. Taylor hoped for.

The events at Ste.-Mère-Église are a perfect example of the confusion that reigned that night. A house fire, probably started by flack shell, was burning on the town *place*. The German commander ordered Mayor Alexandre Renaud to call out his constituents to form a bucket brigade. The fire fighting was in progress when a stick of paratroopers landed in the square and were shot or captured by the Germans — all save Pvt. John Steele, whose parachute hung up on the church steeple and who hung there trying to play dead. Steele was soon taken prisoner, then later released and survived the war.

Meanwhile, Col. Benjamin H. Vandervoort, commanding the 2nd Battalion of the 505th PR, assembled a force north of town, left a platoon under Lt. Turner B. Turnbull, nicknamed "Chief" because of his American Indian ancestry, to create a road block at Neuville, then marched south to aid Col. Edward C. Krause, 3rd Battalion CO. Krause had earlier charged the town with 150 paratroopers, killing or capturing 40 or so of its defenders while being wounded three times himself. Vandervoort, nursing a broken ankle from his hard landing, joined Krause just at

German infantry were mounting a counterattack from the south. Meanwhile to the north, Lt. Turnbull's men held off a counterattack from the 91st Division's 1058th Regiment. Turnbull, later supported by Vandervoort and by gunfire from the battleship *Nevada*'s (a Pearl Harbor survivor) 14-inch main battery, foiled the German efforts. The paratroopers held Ste.-Mère-Église until relieved by elements of the 4th ID moving inland from Utah Beach.

Two "must sees" in Ste.-Mère-Église are the church and the airborne museum. As soon as you exit your car, your eyes are going to be fixed on the church steeple. All summer long, a dummy paratrooper hangs from his chute in the same place that Pvt. Steele came to rest. From the ground, the dummy looks a bit foreshortened, or maybe Steele was a small guy. In any case, the dummy is an eye-catcher. Before you take your eyes off the steeple, notice the pockmarks (spang, in British slang) in the stone made by bullets. Now enter the church to view the two stained glass windows commemorating the airdrop. Our favorite is the one showing the Virgin Mary with paratroopers descending around her. The other, dedicated in 1972, has a figure of St. Michael surrounded by various military insignia and stylized parachutes, and is dedicated to the 82nd Airborne Division.

The entrance to the Airborne Museum is east of the church. It is marked by an NTL signpost and a board announcing its rather complicated opening and closing times: open April – Sept., 0900 – 1845; Feb., Mar., Oct. and Nov., 0930 – 1200 and 1400 – 1800; closed 1 December and 31 January. The museum is certainly worth a visit, if for no other reasons than to walk through the body of a World War II glider and buy a "cricket," one of the clickers than the 101st AD paratroopers used to locate one another in the dark. A memorial to the 505th Parachute Infantry Regiment was dedicated in 1994 and a plaque fastened to a tree commemorates Pvt. William H. Tucker who landed nearby.   Tucker had an interesting post-war career when President John F. Kennedy appointed him to chair the Interstate Commerce Commission, and, after that job, he headed up the Penn Central Railroad.

Pfc. John Steele still hangs from the church steeple in Ste.-Mère-Église

In front of the church, constructed between the 11th and 14th centuries, stands one of the older CD monuments and a plaque to Alexandre Renaud, the town mayor in 1944.

Standing before the Hôtel de Ville, to the south of the church, is a milestone marking "Km 0" on the *Voie de la Liberté*. Behind it is a stone honoring both Generals Gavin and Ridgeway. The American flag that Col. Krause raised over the town on D-Day, and that he had flown earlier over liberated Naples, is displayed inside.

And not to be forgotten, at the far end of the *place*, in the direction from which you entered town, stands the carefully preserved hand pump that was used to provide water to fight the house fire in the early hours of D-Day.

Before you leave Ste.-Mère-Église on N 13 you have to decide whether to drive north to Cherbourg or to return to Bayeux.

If you choose to visit Cherbourg, you had better plan for extra time to make the round trip drive. The distance from Bayeux to Cherbourg is about 100 km or an hour's drive each way. From Ste.-Mère-Église, the distance is about 40 km.

CHERBOURG

Cherbourg, the post D-Day objective of Collin's VII Corps, was considered essential to the success of Operation Overlord because of its port facilities and its proximity to the proposed PLUTO terminal. The port was wrecked by the German defenders and took months to repair. And, the struggle up the Cotentin Peninsula was costly and time-consuming slog for the American Divisions involved. The main points of interest near Cherbourg for those interested in the 1944 invasion are:

- The Fort du Roule and its museum, renovated in 1994 and accessible by lift from the city.

- A plaque on the *Hôtel de Ville* commemorating Sgt. William F. Finlay's liberation of the building on June 26, 1944.

- V-1 launch site at le Mesnil-au-Val, some 5 km southeast of Cherbourg. This site is hard to find.

- Remnants of Atlantic Wall fortifications around the port area and the Hôtel Mercure.

- Ninth Air Force plaque at the Cherbourg airport.

- A plaque on the *Hôtel de Ville* commemorating Sgt. William F. Finlay's liberation of the building on June 26, 1944.

As a special attraction for Civil War buffs, the cemetery at Tourlaville, a few kilometers east of Cherbourg on D 901 holds the graves of the seamen killed in the duel between the USS *Kearsarge* and the CSS *Alabama* on June 19, 1864.

However, if you choose to not to visit Cherbourg, there are a several other sites of interest you may want to visit before you leave the Ste.-Mère-Église area:

- Some 4 km west of Ste.-Mère-Église on D 15 at La Fière, where the road crosses the Merderet River, stands a statue of an American paratrooper "Iron Mike" that was unveiled on June 7, 1997 by Maj. Gen. Kellogg, then commanding the 82nd Airborne. The statue is a replica of one at Ft. Benning, GA. On the bank of the river, about 100 yards from "Iron Mike" is a small sign marking Gen. James Gavin's foxhole from which he directed the fight along this road to block a German advance on Ste.-Mère-Église.

- If you backtrack almost to N 13, then take D 67 to the southwest through Chef du Pont to its crossing of the Merderet you will find a NTL marker and a memorial plaque to the 508th PIR. This spot marks Drop Zone N, the intended landing area of the 508th. Of course, the actual drop spread them over a six-mile-long area.

DRIVING BACK TO BAYEUX...

As you drive back along N 13 toward Bayeux you may want to make three more stops; one at les Forges just 3.5 km south of Ste.-Mère-Église, the second at the La Cambe German Cemetery between Isigny-sur-Mer and Bayeux and the third at Tour-en-Besin.

– You can take D 70 from Chef-du-Pont toward N 13. About 100 yards before you pass under N 13 there is a stone marking the location of U.S. Cemetery #3. The burials here began in June 1944 and the cemetery was closed in 1948, when the remains were either repatriated or reburied at the St. Laurent site.

– Continue on D 70 under N 13 in the direction of Ste. Marie du Mont until you reach the intersection with D 129, and then turn right toward Hiesville. At the second crossroads, stop at the memorial. The brass plaque mounted on this low stone memorial commemorates Brig. Gen. Don F. Pratt who was killed on D-Day when the glider in which he was riding crash-landed here (Landing Zone E). Pratt, second in command of the 101st Airborne, was one of five men killed as many of the 53 Waco gliders landing nearby struck stone fences surrounding the *bocage* fields.

There are also memorials in Hiesville to Gen. Maxwell D. Taylor commemorating the HQ he set up here on June 6.

Return to N 13 and drive past Carentan and Isigny. Some 6 km past Isigny turn into the long tree lined entrance to La Cambe German Military Cemetery.

The grave of German tanker Michael Wittman and his crew at La Cambe

This site was once a burial place for Americans and well as Germans, but once the Americans remains were moved in 1948, the German government took over the operation of La Cambe. Over the years, youths from many nations including Germany came to Normandy on their summer vacations to help with the landscaping, and some still do. Since the new N13 – E 46 four lane road would necessitate a new entrance to the cemetery, the *Volksbund Deutsche Kriegsgräbefürsorge* took the opportunity to transform its entrance. Now you approach La Cambe along a tree lined avenue and can find ample parking next to the new visitor's center. The center maintains a computer data bank that holds the names and locations of all the World War II soldiers buried in Normandy.

The cemetery presents a somber face with its clusters of small red granite crosses and flat stones. In the center of the grounds are shrouded statues standing atop a berm containing the remains of 296 soldiers. The cemetery contains over 21,000 German dead, among them SS Lieutenant Michael Wittmann, the foremost tank ace of the war, buried in Block 47, Row 3, Grave 120. Wittmann's remains were recovered in the 1980s.

Continue on toward Bayeux to complete your tour. On the way you will pass the village of Tour-en-Bessin. A wall off the parking area in the village center displays a plaque to the 1st Infantry Division, the "Big Red One," whose 26th IR liberated the village.

A half a kilometer from Vaucelles, a short distance from Bayeux, you will pass a small roadside stone marking the A 13 airfield built by the 846th Air Engineer Battalion and used by the 373rd and 406th Fighter Groups (P-47s) and the 394th Bombardment Group (B-26s). This memorial was dedicated in 1989 as part of the efforts of the Ninth Air Force Association to mark the Ninth's airfields in Normandy.

As you reach Bayeux notice the bas-relief of Gen. De Gaulle symbolically liberating Bayeux in June 1944.

Slapton Sands Discovery

The Massachusetts company, Hydroid, announced in April 2014 that one of its underwater robotic vehicles had located the wrecks, off Slapton Sands, Devon, of the two American LSTs (Nos. 507 and 531) that were sunk in April of 1944 during Operation Tiger.

Tiger was the third of four training exercise for the upcoming D-Day assault on the Normandy beaches (Operation Neptune).

German high-speed attack craft, Schnellboote, known to the Allies as E-boats, attacked a column of LSTs during the night of 28 April 1944, sinking two and damaging a third. The loss of life in the embarked troops of the 4th U.S. Infantry Division was horrendous, some 456 GIs, ten times the number of men the Division lost landing over Utah Beach on D-Day. Also, 183 naval personnel were lost at Slapton Sands.

This disaster was kept under wraps at the time for security reasons and largely forgotten after the war until Britisher, Ken Small, mounted a campaign to publicize the event. Small's efforts led to the 1984 recovery of a Sherman DD (amphibious) tank sunk off the Sands and the erection, in 1987, of a memorial to the Americans lost in Operation Tiger, featuring that tank, located on the beach at Torcross.

Small's account of the disaster and his recovery efforts are chronicled in his book, "The Forgotten Dead," (London, 1988).

HOW CLOSE WAS THE U.S. ARMY TO FAILURE ON D-DAY?

Historical events always take on the aura of inevitability after the fact. Even to ask the "what if" question is to enter the realm of speculation, even fiction. Still, for the purpose of sparking your interest in touring the Normandy beachheads, let's engage in a little speculation.

THE AIRBORNE ASSAULT

Allied planners placed great faith in airborne operations, even though the use of airborne troops in the Mediterranean theater, especially in the assault on Sicily, had been near disasters. With two American airborne divisions in England, the planners felt they had to devise a scheme that could make effective use of their unique capabilities. But how to use them to the greatest effect, i.e., where to locate the drop zones, bedevilled the planners until the very eve of the invasion.

Early in the planning, when only three infantry divisions were to be landed from the sea, the drop zones (DZs) for the two American airborne divisions were located just south of Bayeux where the airborne troops could block German movement toward the landing beaches. Later, after the seaborne assault was increased to five divisions, the 82nd Airborne Division's DZs were moved to the vicinity of St.-Sauveur-le-Vicomte at the base of the Cotentin Peninsula with the idea that they could block the German reinforcement of Cherbourg, allowing the quick capture of that valuable port. (The 101st Airborne Division's DZs were now firmly in place astride the four exits from Utah Beach, where they remained through D-Day.)

But, when aerial reconnaissance revealed the emplacement of "Rommel asparagus" (upright poles wired together and mined) on Hill 110, the DZ for the 508th Parachute Infantry, and the German 91st Division taking up residence nearby, the 82nd's DZs were moved to the Merderet River valley just west of the town Ste.-Mère-Église barely a week before the scheduled jump.

There were two problems with the 82nd's new DZs. First, the Germans had begun to flood the Merderet River valley, but, because of high grass, the meter-deep water was not visible in aerial reconnaissance photographs. Numerous paratroopers, unable to free themselves from their cumbersome parachute harnesses, drowned D-Day morning in that shallow water. And, if they jumped late, the sticks stood a good chance of landing in the Bay of the Seine, east of the peninsula, with equally fatal results.

The jump itself was a disaster. Flying in tight Vs of Vs, the 347 C-47s carrying the 82nd reached the west coast of the Cotentin in formation and on schedule. Then, they unexpectedly entered a dense cloudbank. Chaos resulted. The tight formations broke up, as the aircraft dove or climbed to avoid mid-air collisions and the flak that the Germans began to throw their way, with the result that the 82nd landed badly scattered. A couple of hour after he came down in a cow pasture, Col. James M. Gavin, commander of the 82nd, had been able to assemble only a hundred men from his command and found them so disorganized that he was unable to accomplish anything other than search for equipment that may have fallen in the swampy water. Unable to withstand a German counterattack, he led his men across the 1,000 yards of water to the hoped for safety of a railroad embankment while the Germans fired at them without hindrance.   Another group of troopers under Col. Ben Vandervoort held the highway north of Ste.-Mère-Église while elements of the 505th and 508th PI under Lt. Col. Charles J. Timmes and the 1st battalion of the 325th Glider Infantry under Lt. Col. Terry Sanford held off the Germans to the south of the town. Very likely the paratroopers would have succumbed to the German counterattacks if help if the form of artillery and tanks had not arrived from Utah Beach.

In fact, one group of some 182 paratroopers from the 507th PI gathered in the village of Graignes, cut off from other American units. The Germans attacked on the 11th, routing the small force. Something like 100 troopers managed to escape to American lines.   The remainder were either killed or captured; some wounded and prisoners were murdered (see our sidebar).

While the casualties on D-Day had amounted to only 10 percent of the Division's strength, by the time the 82nd was withdrawn from combat on July 11th the total killed, wounded and missing had reached 46 percent. The Division wouldn't see combat again until September, spending the interval reconstituting itself in the relative quiet of England.

MASSACRE AT GRAIGNES

The story of what happened in the village of Graignes, south of Carentan, was the nightmare of those who planned the American night-drop – troopers isolated by the drop and defeated before they could make contact with the seaborne invasion.

On the morning of D-Day a sizeable number of paratroopers from the 507th PIR, 82nd AD gathered in the village of Graignes south of Carentan.   They were miles from their drop zone and unable to communicate with their commanders. Aided by the villagers, Maj. Charles D. Johnson of the 3rd Battalion organized a command post and began to harass local German patrols.   Skirmishes with the Germans continued until 11 June, when the enemy attacked Graignes in force. Johnson and his second in command, Lt. Elmer Farnham, were both killed, but the troopers held on until they ran out of ammo. As many as a hundred were able to escape into the countryside. About two-dozen prisoners, some wounded, were shot or bayoneted by the Germans on the 11th and 12th. Numerous villagers, including two priests, were also murdered for aiding the Americans. Before the Germans departed, they virtually destroyed the village and razed its 800-year-old church.

After the war, part of the ruined church was rebuilt as a memorial and on June 12, 1949, it was rededicated with U.S. Ambassador David Bruce in attendance. (Bruce, by the way, was a former OSS officer who had entered France shortly after the invasion.) Two other memorial plaques commemorate the 507th PIR and the individuals, French and American, massacred here.

Graignes can be reached by leaving the N 13 just east of Carentan and taking N 174 south to St. Jean-de-Daye. From there take D 57 west for 5 km to Graignes. The round trip is approximately 32 km.

THE SEABORNE ASSAULT ON OMAHA BEACH

The beach fronting Merville had several strikes against it even before the lousy weather on D-Day nearly wrecked the V Corps landing. First, the beach was apparently chosen, not for its ability to support a landing by two RCTs abreast, but because it was the only suitable beach between the British Gold Beach, directly north of Bayeux, and the mouth of the Vire River. A steep shingle bank made up of softball-sized cobbles that mark high tide on this stretch of beach would have to be breached to allow vehicles to cross. Behind the shingle lay a marshy area that was heavily mined. Above the minefields was a steep bluff covered with brush and cut by a number of draws that the Neptune planners thought could be used by troops to exit the beach. Since the German defenders thought the same way, the draws were heavily fortified with underground bunkers, trenches and assorted pillboxes. On the best of mornings, Omaha Beach was going to be a tough nut to crack. Dawn on June 6, 1944 was not the best of mornings.

Omaha Beach Comité du Débarquement Monument

British historians have long argued that Gen. Omar Bradley's failure to utilize the British "funnies," assorted tanks fitted out with various devices designed to defeat the beach defenses, was a major error on his part. That argument goes something like this – if the V Corps had trained for and used the "funnies" on Omaha, the assault across the shingle, fore-beach and up the bluff would have been accomplished with less confusion and loss of life. In other words, we had paid for our parochialism with the lives of hundreds of GIs and almost brought down the entire invasion effort, because a failure at Omaha would have jeopardized all of Operation Neptune.

First Infantry Division Monument at Omaha Beach

However, the American decision was probably correct. Many of the "funnies," other than the Duplex-Drive (DD) tanks, were based on British tank chassis (mainly Churchills) that would have presented serious training and logistical problems for the Americans. Flame-throwing and petard firing tanks might work wonderfully on pill boxes and machinegun nests located at the water's edge, but we question their usefulness against the German defenses on a large part of Omaha, which were concentrated along the top of the bluff. How were these clumsy British machines going to cross the shingle bank and climb the bluff to engage the enemy emplacements before being knocked out of action? As for the "funnies" carrying fascines and bridging equipment, where were the anti-tank ditches on Omaha in need of spanning? "Flails," M4 Shermans carrying a rotary beater attached to their prows, might have worked on Omaha if they had landed alongside infantry faced with minefields, but that fortunate conjunction would have been unusual given the confusion that morning.

The DD tanks themselves were a clever adaptation of the ubiquitous M-4 "Sherman," the real workhorse of the Allied Armies in all theaters. By fitting two propellers and an upright waterproof-canvas-dam to the hull, General Sir Percy Hobart's designers produced an amphibious tank that could theoretically swim ashore under its own power. But, off Omaha Beach on D-Day the DD tanks were mostly a failure. Launched too far off the beach in heavy seas they were not designed to traverse, most sank on their swim in; they still lie on the bottom of the Bay of the Seine. The American planners' mistake was the decision to launch the Shermans so far from the beach for fear that the LCTs bringing them in would run aground as the tide receded.

The air bombardment plan was faulty as well. No one, including Eisenhower and Montgomery seemed to realize that heavy bombers were almost useless, maybe even dangerous, as close infantry support weapons. The 1,200 heavies (B-17s and B-24s) came in from the sea following, where possible, pathfinder planes using radar to penetrate the cloud cover below. They released their 500 pound bombs from 20,000 feet a few seconds late for fear of hitting the troops now beginning to land on the beach below them. As a result, the German beach defenses were mostly untouched, while Norman cow pastures farther inland were hard hit. Many planes were unable to drop their bombs in the initial attack because of the cloud cover. The planes then returned to England where they were refueled, and then sent on a second mission to bomb Norman towns and other targets miles inland from the beaches.

Actually, the bombing campaign against the French transportation system that the Allied Air Forces had reluctantly conducted in the two months preceding D-Day was more decisive. That campaign had helped isolate the battlefield and had driven the Luftwaffe out of France. But, the price had been high: the campaign had cost the Allies over 2,000 aircraft and 12,000 airmen. On D-Day the results were evident – the Allies flew 56 sorties for every one that the Luftwaffe managed. That maximum effort cost them 113 planes, not one lost to enemy aircraft.

The bombardment from the sea was no more effective. It consisted mainly of a rocket barrage slated for H Hour-10 that did little damage to the beach defenses. In fact most of the wire, mine fields and gun emplacements were untouched by the massive amounts of ordnance thrown their way that morning. Infantrymen in the first waves were shot to pieces before they ever reached the beach when their landing craft grounded on offshore sand bars. Only later did they learn that the German 352nd Division, a well-trained and equipped unit, had moved into position behind Omaha Beach only weeks before the landing. GI's of the 16th and 116th RCTs were saved by their own dogged courage, slow German reaction (the 352nd Division was committed to the battle piecemeal) and from the close fire support they received from the Allied destroyers patrolling inshore

In his recent monograph, *Omaha Beach: A Flawed Victory*, Adrian Lewis placed the blame for the debacle squarely on the shoulders of the senior Overlord commanders, Eisenhower, Bradley and Montgomery. Lewis maintains that all three (and, by inference, their staffs as well) were too enamored with strategic airpower. Having fought a nasty intra-service battle to gain control of the Allies' strategic air assets, Neptune planners thought it was imperative that they be used to support the sea-born landing. Ignoring American experience in the Pacific and British experience in the Mediterranean with combined operations, the Neptune plan relied too heavily on accurate bombing from 20,000 feet, followed by a short naval bombardment, to destroy the German beach defenses. Even on a calm, clear morning the heavy bombers of the American Eighth Air Force and the British Bomber Command could not have accomplished that mission, and bombing accurately by radar through cloud cover was completely beyond their capabilities in 1944. High altitude precision bombing was a myth perpetrated by air power advocates. It was unfortunate that the Neptune plan relied on it so heavily.

THE VICTORY AT UTAH BEACH

The landings on Utah Beach fared much better than its counterpart on Omaha. Medium bombers of the Ninth Air Force, streaming across the beach at 500 feet, bombed with much more accuracy than did the heavies across the bay. In fact, the German positions at La Madeleine (strong point WN-5) were so completely disrupted by the 250-pound bombs rained on them from the B-26 Marauders and A-20 Havocs that the first wave of the 8th Infantry coming ashore there, two miles south of its designated landing areas, met minimal resistance. The Assistant Divisional Commander, Brig. Gen. Theodore Roosevelt, Jr., Col. James A. Van Fleet, commanding the 8th Infantry, and some staff

90th Division Monument at Utah Beach

members quickly made the decision to land the follow up waves at La Madeleine. In short order Van Fleet's 2nd and 3rd Battalions gained control of Exits 1 and 2 that ran through Pouppeville and Ste.-Marie-du-Mont. By nightfall, GIs from Utah Beach had cut N 13 at Les Forges, south of Ste-Mère-Église, and had made contact with paratroopers from the 101st PID. As luck would have it, the defenses at the badly damaged WN-5 strongpoint were much weaker than those at Les Dunes de Varreville where the landings originally were to have occurred. Also, the presence of the American paratroopers at the landward end of the roads exiting the beach delayed any counterattack by the German 6th Parachute Regiment located at Carentan. The 4th ID suffered fewer than 200 casualties on D-Day, less by a factor of almost twenty than the number it had experienced at the Slapton Sands training exercise in late April. The one conspicuous failure at Utah Beach on D-Day was the inability of the Navy to silence the heavy German guns firing from casements near St.-Marcouf. Apparently, neither sea nor air power was able to accomplish the mission, so it eventually fell to the infantry to put the battery out of commission.

GOLD, JUNO AND SWORD BEACHES, BRITISH LANDING ZONES

TOUR

Once again, we assume that you have access to an automobile for this tour and that you are based in Bayeux. If that is the case, you will want again to take D 6 from the Bayeux traffic loop to Port-en-Bessin where you will turn east on D 514, a road that will conveniently take you along the three British Second Army Beaches and also lead you to the Pegasus Bridge and the Merville Battery, where memorable battles were fought on D-Day by British airborne forces. The entire distance is approximately 54 km.

High bluffs, hiding German gun emplacements, dominate the small beaches from Port-en-Bessin to Arromanches-les-Bains, forcing the landings on Gold Beach eastward between Le Hamel and La Rivière. There, the bluffs recede and give way to open beaches. Beyond Courseulles-sur-Mer, low hills give way to the valleys of the Seulles and Orne rivers. From St.-Aubin-sur-Mer, D 514 leads you through an almost continuous line of seaside resorts until you reach Ouistreham-Riva Bella. Parking along this section of the road is often limited. Given the number of monuments, memorials and museums found over these 54 km, it is probably wise to allot no less than two days to traverse the whole. Virtually everywhere the Germans built strongpoints (Wiederstandnester) you can find weathered bunkers, casemates and gun emplacements of various types. Some are open; most are not. We point out many of the most obvious ones, but you will stumble upon many more if you look for them.

PORT-IN-BESSIN
For the tour of Port-en-Bessin see the beginning section of the tour of Omaha Beach.

GOLD BEACH
As you arrive at Port-en-Bessin, turn left (east) on D 514. You are now at the western edge of Gold Beach where the 50th Northumbrian Division landed on D-Day.

Longues Battery
Continue east for 5 km to the turnoff to the Longues Battery, which is marked by a CD monument. This massive battery of four casemated 155-mm naval guns was controlled from a fortified bunker on the cliff's face. The battery was repeatedly bombed and damaged before D-Day. Nevertheless, it managed to straddle the HMS *Bulolo*, the XXX Corps command ship, before being put out of action by fire from HMS *Ajax* and the French cruiser *Georges Leygues*. Today, much of the battery has been restored.

Follow the signs to the observation table on the cliff. From that position you can see the command post (now off limits for safety reasons) and examine the table that indicates the relative position of the bombardment force.

Continue on D 514 a short distance to Arromanches-les-Bain. As you enter the town, notice that a memorial to the Forces Aériennes Françaises Libres stands on the side of the large bus parking area.

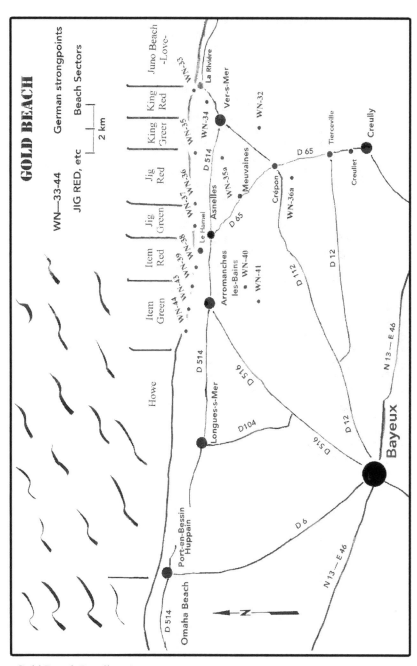

Gold Beach Landing Areas

Arromanches-les-Bains

The Overlord planners chose Arromanches as the site for one of the two Mulberries (Mulberry B), the artificial ports planted offshore to handle the movement of supplies before established ports could be captured. The remains of Mulberry B still dominate the Arromanches seascape.

In Arromanches, follow the signs that lead you to the Musée du Débarquement, a museum that occupies a modern building along the seawall with an array of Allied flags flying overhead. This museum, one of the more interesting of the D-Day museums, is open daily May through August from 0900 to 1900. Opening times vary for the remainder of the year. Check the Museum's website (www.musee-arromanches.fr) for updated details. Admission charged.

It is possible to climb the steep bluff to the east of the museum to reach an orientation platform that provides a superlative view of the port and Mulberry B. The site can also be reached by driving from Arromanches on D514 and parking nearby. At the top of the bluff a Sherman tank sits not far from a German radar station. Nearby bunkers were silenced by fire from HMS *Belfast*, now permanently moored in the Thames near central London. The radar station, known as *Stützpunkt Arromanches*, is today the site of Arromanches 360-degree Cinema that shows a 20-minute film, "The Price of Liberty," every 30 minutes. It is open daily 0930-1840 June through August; 1000-1840 February through May and September through December. Closed in January. Tel: +33(0)2.31.22.30.30. Admission charged.

MULBERRIES

The Mulberries were the brainchild of Winston Churchill, who wrote in his memoirs that he had first conceived the idea in 1917 when he served in Lloyd George's cabinet as First Lord of the Admiralty.

A quarter century later his idea came to fruition in the two Mulberries actually emplaced off Omaha and Gold Beaches. Mulberry A, the remains of which are still visible off Omaha Beach, was destroyed by the storm of 19-21 June, while Mulberry B at Arromanches continued to unload men, equipment and supplies for months after the landings, some 500,000 tons in all, before being abandoned after Cherbourg and smaller ports came into use.

Both structures were essentially the same and composed of several elements — Gooseberries (outer, floating breakwaters), Phoenixes (concrete caissons), derelict ships sunk to protect the perimeter of the port, pier-heads that could rise and fall on the tides with floating metal piers connecting them to the beach. Note: Gooseberries, composed mainly of derelict ships, were put in place off most of the beaches.

Asnelles and Le Hamel

Continue for 2 km to Asnelles where, near the Place Alexander Stanier (named after the commander of the 231st Brigade), there are memorials to the 2nd South Wales Borderers, a unit of the 56th Brigade that was then attached to the 50th Division, and further east a memorial to the Brigade itself. Off the Rue The Devonshire Regiment you will find a memorial to the 50th (Northumbrian) Infantry Division. Nearby is a memorial commemorating De Gaulle's June 14 speech to the people of France. Drive down to the beach along the Rue de Southampton and stop in the car park near the massive blockhouse, which was part of WN-37.

In front of you is boundary between the Jig Green (west) and the Item Red sectors of Gold Beach where the 231st British Infantry Brigade (consisting of the 1st Battalions of the Hampshire and Dorset Regiments and the 2nd Battalion of the Devonshire Regiment) landed. The assault did not go well. WN-37 had not been significantly touched by the pre-landing bombardment. Because of high seas, the commander of the LCT flotilla decided to land his tanks directly on the beach after the engineers and infantry had landed, leaving them unsupported in the meantime. As the drama played out, one LCT, badly hit off shore, was unable to land its tanks. Some of the armor that was landed from the remaining LCTs bogged down in the sand and clay of the beach. The Hampshires took the brunt of the fire from the 75-mm gun in the blockhouse as well as fire from WN-36 to the east. This one gun accounted for three of the four flail-equipped Sherman tanks (Crabs) that had landed here. The fourth Crab made it into the village before being knocked out. A plaque on the blockhouse credits this single gun with six British tanks. Note the plaque to the 147th Field Regiment, part of the 8th Armoured Brigade that came ashore nearby. Also, take note of the "Tobruk," a small, fortified gun pit at the east end of the car park. Eventually neutralizing the blockhouse with help from well-placed shots from an AVRE (a Churchill tank mounting a petard), and bypassing other German positions, the Hampshires fought their way inland.

Further to the east, the 1st Dorset's LCAs, swept further east than had been intended, were not subject to the fire from Le Hamel, thus the men got ashore with fewer casualties. However, that left it to the 1st Hampshires to neutralize WN-36 before aiding in the attack on WN-37. Soon specialized armor belonging to the 8th Armoured Brigade opened up three beach exits allowing the Dorsets to advance south to engage units of the German 352nd Division along the Arromanches ridge near Ryes.

By walking a half-mile west along the beach road (Boulevard de la Mer) from the car park you can reach WN-38 and another half-mile beyond that WN-39. WN-38 was forced to surrender by the combined actions of a company of the 1st Hampshires and Lance-Sergeant Scaife's ubiquitous AVRE that earlier had been instrumental in the capture of WN-37.

Major John Littlejohn's D Company of the 1st Hampshires neutralized WN-39 during the afternoon of D-Day.

THE CREULLET CHÂTEAU DETOUR

General Montgomery set up his tactical HQ in Creullet château after he came ashore. It was here that he met with the PM and Field-Marshal Smuts on 12 June and with George VI four days later. On 22 June Monty moved his HQ to Blay, west of Bayeux, to be nearer the American beaches.

To reach the château, take the Avénue du 6 Juin from Asnelles, and then follow D 65 east though Meuvaines and Crépon, where here is a stunning memorial to the Green Howards at the D 112 intersection with D 65. The memorial is on your left. The stone on which a bronze statue of a seated soldier stands list the names of the 179 Green Howards who died in Normandy, 28 of whom were casualties on D-Day.

Continue on through Tierceville where there is a restored, cement copy of the Eros statue in Piccadilly Circus originally created by the 179 Special Field Company of the Royal Engineers in August 1944.

Just beyond the junction with D 12 and the village of Creullet you will come upon a Y junction. The château is to your right down a short narrow road. If you cross the Seulles River, you have gone too far. The total distance is about 7 or 8 km.

In the town of Creully, just across the river, there is a memorial to the 4th/7th Dragoon Guards who landed with DD tanks and various other ARVEs along with the Green Howards on King sector of Gold Beach. The BBC maintained a broadcast studio inside the tower of the château, now the *mairie*. Ask at the *mairie* if it possible to see those artifacts.

La Rivière and Ver-sur-Mer

La Rivière marks the eastern edge of Gold Beach. A monument to the 2d Battalion of the Hertfordshire Regiment stands in the Espace Robert Kiln near the crossroads where D 514 intersects the Avenue de 6 Juin (D 112). Also, take notice of the Sexton self-propelled gun, the Porpoise ammunition sled and the plaque on the gatepost of the house next to the pharmacy indicating that Adm. Bertram Ramsay RN, Allied Naval C-in-C, used it briefly as his HQ.

Turn onto D112 and drive into Ver-sur-Mer about 1 km to the Musée America Gold Beach.

This museum derives its odd name from the fact that weather conditions forced Cmdr. Richard E. Byrd to ditch his Fokker Tri-motor *America* in the sea off Ver-sur-Mer after his epic transatlantic flight of 31 June-1 July 1927. Quite possibly Byrd was lost and certainly late; Charles Lindbergh had made the same flight alone earlier that year in *The Spirit of St. Louis*. Byrd and his three crewmembers survived. Today, this excellent museum is also dedicated to retelling the story of the assault over Gold Beach. The museum is open daily in July and August from 1030 to 1730. The times are the same in April, May, June, September and October, but the museum is closed on Tuesdays. It is closed from November through March, except by prior arrangement.   Tel: +33 (0) 2.31.22.58.58; Fax: +33 (0) 2.31.21.09.12; www.goldbeachmusee.org.uk

After leaving the museum, retrace your route back to the crossroads. At that position, WN-33 is directly north of you and defines the eastern edge of King Red Beach. To your left about 2 km distant is WN-35. Le Paisty Vert, half way between the two strongpoints, lies on the dividing line between King Red and King Green Beaches. (WN-34 occupied the ground around the lighthouse to the south.)

Cross D 514 and walk down to the beach. To your west is an octagonal gun emplacement that housed a 50-mm gun beyond which is an 88-mm gun casemate that knocked out two AVREs on D-Day.

If you desire, you can walk west along the beach about three-quarters of a kilometer to le Paisty Vert where D Company of the 6th Green Howards landed.

The landings along King Green proceeded relatively smoothly, although both assault companies took casualties on their run in to the beach. Nine frogmen preceded the three LCTs carrying various types of specialized armor, including 19 DD tanks. The LCTs were quickly followed by 10 LCAs bringing in two companies (A and D) of the 6th Green Howards, engineers and a forward artillery observation team.

What happened next is the stuff of D-Day legend. For conspicuous bravery in leading his company in the move inland to attack German positions near Mont Fleury, Major R. Lofthouse was awarded the Military Cross. However, his Company Sergeant Major (CSM), Stan Hollis, received the Victoria Cross, Britain's highest military award and the only one awarded for D-Day heroism. Hollis singlehandedly charged a pillbox under fire disabling it with a grenade and bursts from his Sten gun. Later that day, near the village of Crépon, Hollis attempted to engage an enemy gun emplacement with a PIAT anti-tank weapon. After the gun was destroyed, the wounded CSM openly charged the German position to attract small arms fire so that two of his men could escape from a partially destroyed house where they were trapped. Hollis survived the war to die in the early 1970s. Tonie and Valmai Holt, in their guide to the D-Day landings, state that his VC was sold in 1983 for £32,000.

This completes your tour of Gold Beach. Continue to drive east on D 514 to tour Sword and Juno Beaches, the Pegasus Bridge landing area and the Merville Battery.

JUNO BEACH

The 3rd Canadian Division, commanded by Maj. Gen. R.F.L. Keller, was scheduled to assault Juno Beach at 0745 hours. The assaulting troops came from the 7th and 8th Canadian Infantry Brigades: The Royal Winnipeg Rifles, The Regina Rifle Regiment, The Canadian Scottish Regiment (1st Battalion), The Queens Own Rifles of Canada, Le Régiment de la Chaudiére and The North Shore (New Brunswick) Regiment. Supporting them were the 10th Armoured Regiment (Fort Gary Horse) and the 6th Armoured Regiment (1st Hussars), both riding DD tanks.

Graye-sur-Mer

Continue along D 514 eastward for 5 km. About 150 yards before you reach the bridge over the Seulles River, turn north (left) onto a road that leads down to the beach. A sign marks the turn. Park near the Churchill AVRE tank.

This is the approximate location where PM Winston Churchill, accompanied by General Jan Christian Smuts and Field Marshal Alan Brooke, landed on 12 June 1944 for a tour of the beachhead and lunch with General Montgomery. King George VI came ashore here four days later. A CD monument commemorates these arrivals as well as the D-Day assault.

Churchill and George VI had originally hoped to observe the landings from one of the command ships off shore, but were dissuaded from this plan by their military advisors.

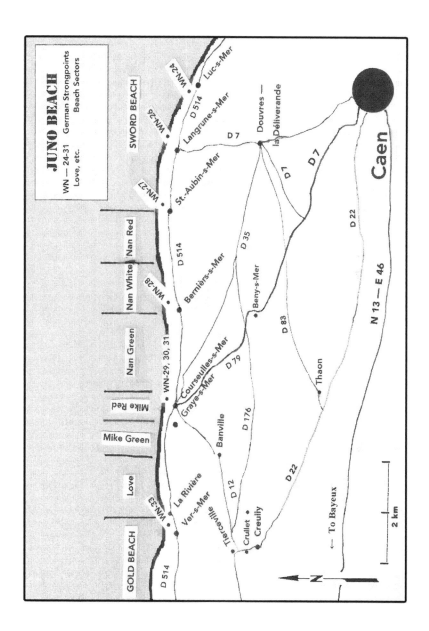

The ARVE you see before you, commanded by Bill Dunn,
became stuck in a flooded culvert and was abandoned. It was
later covered over to make a roadway across the culvert and not
rediscovered until 1974 when it was dug out. Dunn and another

crewmember who also survived the war attended the dedication ceremony.

Also note the large metal Cross of Lorraine standing nearby that commemorates General Charles De Gaulle's arrival in France on June 16. Adm. Philippi De Gaulle dedicated the cross on that date in 1990.

Courseulles-sur-Mer

Return to D 514 and then drive across the Seulles River bridge into the town of Courseulles. Signs will direct you to the port area where there are a number of D-Day memorials. Park near the DD tank. You are standing at the junction of Nan Green (to the east) and Mike Beaches. C Company of the Canadian Scottish Regiment landed on Mike Beach, a kilometer to the west.

This Sherman DD tank (now renamed BOLD), belonging to the 1st Canadian Hussars, was one of five (out of 19) that foundered on its swim into the beach. It was recovered from the seafloor in 1971. Note the duplex drive at the rear (minus the propeller shafts). The lip extending around the entire hull along with upright metal stanchions held the canvas dam that provided buoyancy (of course, it failed in this instance).

Those DD tanks making it ashore provided vital fire support to Company A of the Regina Rifles who had encountered heavy fire from both WN-31, to your immediate front, and from German artillery positions further inland.

A memorial to officers and men of the Regina Rifles who were lost during the war stands by the beach exit. Nearby plaques commemorate De Gaulle's arrival on June 14 and the 1st Canadian Scottish Regiment. There is another memorial to the French destroyer *la Combattante*, built in Scotland in 1942 and lost at sea on February 23, 1945. Further to the west is an impressive, upright, wooden dagger commemorating the "Little Black Devils," the Royal Winnipeg Rifles.

Walk a short distance east to visit the Juno Beach Centre (on the Voie des Français Libres) housed in a stunning modern building done in the Frank Gehry style. This cultural center, opened by the Canadian non-profit Juno Beach Centre Association in 2003, presents the entire Canadian war effort, military and civilian, on the every front where Canadians fought. It also contains exhibits on contemporary Canadian society. Through 2015, the Centre will feature an exhibit entitled, "Grandma, what was it like during the War? Life for Normans and Canadians from occupation to Liberation." The Centre also provides tours of the landing beaches. Tel: +33. (0)2.31.37.32.17; Fax: (+33).(0)2.31.37.83.69; Email: contact@junobeach.org; Website: www.junebeach.org.

Bernières-sur-Mer

Drive east along D 514 for 3 km to Bernières. Park near the CD monument on the beach (Place de 6 Juin). In front of you is the Nan White sector of June Beach where the 8th Canadian Brigade (the Queen's Own Rifles and La Chaudière regiments) landed. The QOR were to have landed behind DD tanks, but high seas breaking over the offshore reefs meant that the Shermans had to be brought to the beach after the infantry was ashore. The nasty weather also meant that the assault companies of the QOR were a half-hour late and some 200 yards east of their designated landing area. The LCAs were forced to drop their bow ramps among the beach obstacles where a fourth were either damaged or sunk. One company of the QOR took 65 casualties attempting to cross the 200 yards to the seawall. However, aided by a flak ship firing from close inshore, the Canadians overran the resistance nests so that when the Régiment de la Chaudière landed a quarter of an hour later, German fire had been largely suppressed.

There a number of memorial plaques and monuments in Bernièrs, most close to the CD monument that sits near the German defensive position (WN-28) or the nearby tourist office. There are several filled in concrete gun positions abutting the seawall. Many of the memorials below are located in an area now named le Place de Canada.

Commemorative plaques to the Queen's Own Rifles, the 5th Hackney Battalion and the No. 3 Beach Group are attached to a Tobruk mortar pit.

- Fort Gary Horse, 10th Armoured Regiment stele.

- Plaque commemorating the French Canadians of La Chaudière Regiment.

- A stele commemorating all Canadian soldiers, sailors and airmen who won the fight for Juno Beach.

- A small rock stele commemorating Canadian soldiers who died on these beaches on D-Day.

- A plaque on a nearby house (288 La Chaudière Regiment street) indicating that it was the HQ for British and Canadian journalists and photographers.

- A plaque to the North Nova Scotia Highlanders on the wall of the lifesaving station near the Tourist Office (to the west of the Place de 6 Juin).

- A plaque on the nearby half-timbered Norman house indicating that it was liberated by soldiers from The Queen's Own Rifles on D-Day after heavy fighting.

- There is a stained glass window in the Notre-Dame Church dedicated to Ernest W. Parker of the Royal Army Signal Corps who landed with The Queen's Own Rifles.

- A stele, commemoration the memory of nine soldiers of the 14th Field Regiment of the Royal Canadian Artillery killed here on D-Day, stands along side D 79A at the southern exit of town toward Bény-sur-mer.

St.-Aubin-sur-Mer

Drive east on D 514 to St.-Aubin-sur-Mer (2 km), and then take the beach road (D 814). The 48th Royal Marine Commando of the 4th Special Service Brigade landed here to secure the east flank of the Canadians landing on Juno Beach. The resistance nest in the town fell only after a costly fight. Not until the seventh were the commandos able to move east to Langrune, where they liked up with the 41st RMC. The 41st had landed on the Queen sector of Sword Beach, and then moved west to make contact with the 48th RMC. These beaches were generally considered too small to support larger landing forces, yet were needed to link up the British and Canadian beaches.

Memorials to the North Shore (New Brunswick) Regiment and the 48th RMC stand near the German blockhouse (WN-27) that still houses its 50-mm anti-tank gun. The monument also recalls the landing of Maurice Duclos, General De Gaulle's emissary, on August 4, 1944. A stele to the Fort Gary Horse can be found about one hundred yards further along the beach road near the Syndicate d'Initiative.

SWORD BEACH
Langrune-sur-Mer

Continue east on D 814 (the beach road) for 2 km to Langrune where there is another memorial commemorating the 48th Royal Marine Commando on one side and the word "Souviens-Toi" (Remember), under the coat of arms of Langrune and the Croix de Guerre, on the other.

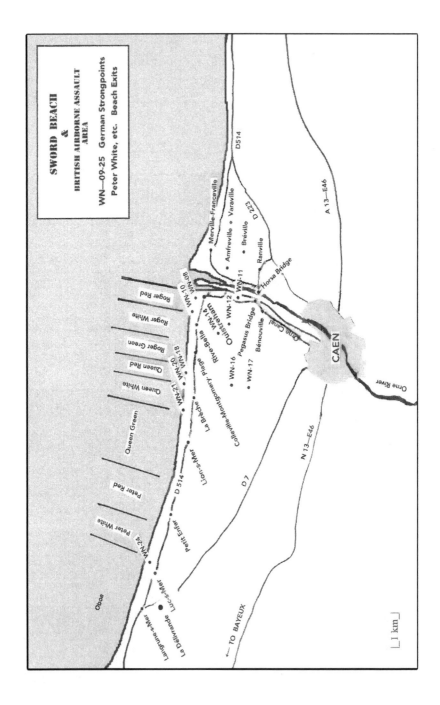

Luc-sur-Mer

Continue east on the beach road (D 514) to Luc (1.5 km). Drive past the casino and look for a small park on the north side of the highway. Park nearby.

The task of capturing the strong point at Le Petit-Enfer (WN-24), near where you are parked, was the job of the 46th Royal Marine Commando that came ashore on June 7. After capturing WN-24, the Commando moved inland to the village of La Dèlivrande.

About a half-mile east of the casino stands an all-purpose stone memorial commemorating on one side the 1st British Commando that landed here on a raid on September 28, 1941 and the liberation of Luc in June 1944. The obverse side commemorates French soldiers and sailors who died for their country.

Lion-sur-Mer

Return to D 514 upon leaving Luc and continue east for 6 km to Lion-sur-Mer. WN-21, codenamed "Trout" is located on the eastern edge of Lion, next to a modern caravan park. This position was the objective of the 41st RMC landing to the east at la Brèche d'Hermanville over the Queen White sector of Sword Beach.

There are a number of memorials in the place near the tourist office including a memorial to the midget submarines that marked the beach perimeters on D-Day, a memorial to the British 3rd Infantry Division, a plinth naming the ships sunk to form the Gooseberry artificial harbour and also giving the order of the assault waves. Finally, there are separate monuments to the 1st South Lancashires and to the regiments of the Royal Artillery attached to the 3rd ID.

A Centaur tank (A27M Cromwell) attached to the 41st RMC is parked just off D 514 in la Brèche. The Queen White and

Queen Red beach sectors extend from the tank eastward to the CD monument at Colleville-Montgomery Plage. Across these sectors the 41st RMC, the 1st South Lancs, the 2nd East Yorks and the 1st Special Service Brigade landed in separate waves on D-Day.

Colleville-Montgomery Plage

Continue east along D 514 to the intersection with the Avenue du 4ème Commando. A statue of Field Marshal Montgomery stands just to the south of the highway. Turn north onto the Avenue du 4ème Commando and drive to the stele on the beach.

There are two memorials at this location, one on either side of the road. One is a memorial to Capitaine Philippe Kieffer, commander of the French contingent of the No. 10 Inter Allied Commando, who was wounded on D-Day. The other memorial marks a temporary British gravesite, the decision to change the village's name to Colville-Montgomery in honor of the Field Marshal and the British/French cooperation in the composition of the No. 4 Commando.

You are now at the location of WN-18. The landing area of the 1st Special Service Brigade is just to your west. This Brigade was composed of the Nos. 3, 4 (with two troops of French Commandos [No. 10] attached) and 6 Army Commandos along with the No. 45 RMC, all under the command of Brigadier Lord Lovat. The job assigned to these commandos, landing behind the first assault waves was to eliminate the casino strong point (WN-10) at Riva-Bella and attack the defences at Ouistreham, before moving inland to make contact with the glider forces holding the bridges across the Orne River and Canal.

The commandos managed to fight their way through Riva Bella, but were stopped by fire from the casino and its adjoining summerhouse. The honor of reducing the German defences in the casino strongpoint was given to Kieffer's French commandos, but they were too lightly armed to make much progress until Kieffer managed to roundup a DD tank. Only after the tank moved up from the beach to provide fire support, were the French able to overcome WN-10, thus allowing the 4 Commando to move inland toward the Orne bridges.

The present casino was rebuilt on the site of the pre-war casino; the Germans levelled that earlier building during the construction of the strongpoint.

Strongpoints Hillman and Morris

While you are in Colleville-Montgomery Plage, you might consider an interesting side tour that will take you away from the beach landing areas to visit strongpoints WN-16 and WN-17, codenamed "Morris" and "Hillman" respectively. To reach these positions you will need to take D 60a south west out of Colleville-Montgomery Plage through the town of Colleville-Montgomery. As you are leaving the town, the road takes an abrupt turn to the west and then turns southwest again. At the second turn, continue straight ahead (west) a short distance on the Rue du Clos Moulin to strongpoint Morris. The casemates that once housed a 100-mm battery are now within the confines of a private riding academy.

Morris was one of the objectives of the 1st Suffolks (8th Infantry Brigade) who had come ashore near la Brèche de Hermanville. There was no firefight; just as the British infantry prepared to blow the wire surrounding the emplacement, the 67 shell-shocked defenders surrendered.

Hillman was a tougher nut to crack. After taking the surrender of Morris without suffering a casualty, the 1st Suffolks moved south to attack Hillman. The attack began a little after 1300 on D-Day. Only after a gap was blown in the section of the minefield, were the Suffolks able to break into the position and not until 2000 hours did the defenders surrender.

Retrace your route to the D 60a intersection with the Rue des Marronniers, and then turn southwest and drive .7 km to the Hillman site. Road signs in Colleville mark the route. There is free parking in the lot beside the concrete bunker.

One of the two plaques on the bunker commemorates the Suffolks who fell here and in the liberation of Europe. The second describes the Hillman complex and its capture. There is an orientation table on top of the bunker.

Hillman, designed as a regimental command post, occupied some 47 acres and is comprised of 18 concrete bunkers (including three Regelbau 608 and a Regelbau 605 bunkers along with three Tobruk H58c gun emplacements) connected by trenches, two belts of concertina wire and a minefield.

Madam Lenauld, the landowner, donated the Hillman site to the Suffolk Regiment in 1989. Since that time it has been maintained by Les Amis du Suffolk Régiment. The site is open on 6 June and Monday through Saturday, 1 July-30 August, 1000-1200 and 1430-1830. There are 2-hour guided tours at 3 pm on Tuesdays, July through September. Check with the Colleville tourist office and the www.amis-du-suffolk-reg.com website for further information.

Ouistreham — Riva-Bella

Return Colleville-Montgomery Plage and continue driving east on D 514 until you reach the Avenue de Bruxelles, turn toward the beach and then continue east along the sea front until you reach a small memorial garden that surrounds a striking flame-like sculpture built atop a steel turret. Park nearby.

This site was part of the Riva-Bella casino strongpoint. The turret housed two machine guns with a 360° field of fire. This memorial commemorates the French commandos killed in the attack on the casino position with their names inscribed on the small stones scattered around the memorial garden.

The Musée du Commando No. 4 occupies the building across the street from the memorial garden, just past the Hôtel le St-Georges. The museum's exhibits emphasize the fighting near here and feature a scale model of the casino strongpoint. Open every day from mid-March to late-October, 1030-1300 and 1330-1830. Tel: +33(0) 2.31.96.63.10. Web: www.muse-4commando.com. Admission charged.

There is another small museum, the Musée le Mur de l'Atlantique, about 200 yards to the east along the Avenue du 6 Juin. Limited parking is available.

Note the 88-mm gun and the V-1 flying bomb outside the museum. The building itself, still painted white, was the control-center for the coastal defence batteries guarding the mouth of the Orne River and Canal. The lightly armed No. 4 Commando attacked the position on D-Day, but it held out until sappers blew the entrance door three days later, after which the 52 occupants quickly surrendered. The tower has now been fully restored and contains interesting exhibits related to its original function on each of its six floors. Open every day 1000-1800, 1 February to 31 December; 0900-1900, 1 April to 30 September. Phone: +33(0) 2.31.97.28.69; Fax: +33(0) 2.31.96.66.05. Email: bunkermusee@aol.com. Admission charged.

BRITISH AIRBORNE LANDING ZONES

To reach the site of the original swing-bridge over the Orne Canal (known as the Pegasus Bridge after the winged-horse badge of the British 6th Airborne Division) take D 514 south out of Ouistreham-Riva Bella for 4 km, and then take the exit to the right that will lift you over the highway on which you were just traveling. Continue straight through the roundabout and across the canal over its new bridge, and then turn left into the Mémorial Pegasus car park.

Mémorial Pegasus

A select force, composed of men from 2d Battalion, Oxfordshire and Buckinghamshire Light Infantry and the Royal Engineers, commanded by Major John Howard of the Ox and Bucks, were given the daunting task of capturing the bridges over the Orne River and Canal. Six Horsa gliders were to carry Howard's force in a nighttime *coup de main* on the two bridges. In an outstanding navigational feat, three glider pilots were able to crash land (the best term describing a WWII military glider's return to earth) within 50 yards of the canal bridge. The lone German sentry who heard the crash failed to sound the alarm because he assumed a bomber had crashed nearby. While one of Howard's squads charged across the bridge, taking only a single casualty, Lt. Den Brotheridge, others overran nearby German defences before the surprised defenders could man their positions. Within minutes of their landing, the Ox and Bucks had captured the bridge and its defences.

The attack on the Orne River Bridge went almost as smoothly although only one of the three gliders assigned to that objective came down near the bridge. The 20-odd men from that lone glider rushed the bridge defences and the surprised defenders, not knowing the odds, scattered before charge.

The bridges had been taken with a total of 16 casualties — two killed, 14 wounded.

Not only had the bridges been captured easily, but they were intact as well, fulfilling the mission of keeping open a link between the British Airborne forces jumping to the east and the infantry and commandos landing on Sword Beach. Both bridges were wired for demolition, but no charges had been placed.

British Horsa Glider on display at Mémorial Pegasus

Howard's men held the bridges through D-Day in the face of sporadic German counter-attacks. One such counterattack soon developed as two armoured vehicles, followed by infantry, clanked down D 514 from Bénoville toward the bridge. Howard, anticipating a counterattack from that direction, had positioned Sergeant "Wagger" Thornton in a forward location with a PIAT, a clumsy, short-range, anti-tank weapon. Thornton's shot knocked out the lead vehicle causing the attackers to break off.

Around 1200 hours, some two and a half minutes after they were to have been reinforced, the defenders were startled by the distant sound of bagpipes. The 1st Special Service Brigade, led by Brigadier Lord Lovat, had arrived with its piper, Bill Millin. The two forces joined ranks to the tune of "Blue Bonnets over the Border" and the crack of small arms fire. Although the Orne bridges were not truly secure until units of the 3rd British ID arrived late in the afternoon, the skirl of Millin's pipes had reassured Howard's beleaguered men that the seaborne landings had succeeded. The commandos took casualties as they dashed across the bridge, but regrouped and continued toward their objectives further to the east.

The first thing you should do after arriving is visit the museum itself, housed in a modern building, which is devoted to retelling the history of the British airborne assault. Its use of models, artefacts and memorabilia (including Bill Millin's bagpipe) is outstanding and should not be missed. The museum is open every day February through March, 1000-1700; April through September, 0930-1830 and October through 15 December, 1000-1700. Tel: +33(0) 2.31.78.19.44; FAX: +33(0) 2.31.78.19.42; Email: info@memorial-pegasus.org. Admission charged.

Pegasus Bridge where it rests today

The original Orne canal swing-bridge rests just behind the museum building. This bridge, opened in 1933, was removed in 1993 to make way for a longer, more modern structure. The old bridge sat somewhat neglected until 2000, when it was moved to the location it now occupies in time for the dedication of Mémorial Pegasus.

The site itself abounds with memorabilia connected to the glider assault, including a full-scale replica of a Horsa glider and a British artillery piece, among other outdoor exhibits.

A recently recovered and restored Centaur tank attached to one of the Royal Marine Commandos was dedicated on 5 June 2014. This tank replaces one recovered in 1975 at la Brèche d'Hermanville that had been on display here since 1977. That earlier Centaur is presumably the one now located at la Brèche.

The original bridge itself makes a spectacular monument, flanked by an older CD monument and an array of flags. There are stone markers just to the south marking the landing sites of the three gliders carrying Major John Howard's assault force.

Other sites of interest found nearby and part of the Mémorial Pegasus today include:

- A stone cross commemorating the liberation at the Bénouville crossroads.

- The Café Gondrée stands at the western end of the new bridge and proudly claims to be the first house liberated in France. M. Georges Gondrée and his wife Thérèse had in fact provided intelligence on the German defenses prior to D-Day and champagne to their liberators after D-Day. After a family legal squabble in 1988, the cafe remained in the hands of their daughter, Arlette Gondrée-Pritchett, who has kept the cafe open as a shrine to Howard's men who liberated it. Today, the cafe houses a small museum and gift shop, and is generally open from

April through November. For more information contact M. Gondrée-Prichett, Tel/Fax: +33 (0) 2.31.44.62.25.

Café Gondree still operates as it did in 1944

- A memorial stone along the canal bank marking the site of a "Bailey bridge," London 1, built here on D-Day+3.

- An actual Bailey bridge.

- A statue of Major Howard.

- A marker commemorating the link up between the No. 6 Commando and Major Howard's force. In 1984, Bill Millin was photographed next to this marker that depicts him with his bagpipes on D-Day.

Walk back toward Bénouville from the Café Gondrée to the roundabout to view a memorial to the 7th Parachute Regiment. A plaque on the Bénouville mairie, across the roundabout, proclaims that it was the first town hall in France to be liberated.

Horsa Bridge

After its capture on D-Day, the bridge over the Orne River became known as the Horse Bridge. It is possible to reach it by foot from the Mémorial Pegasus by walking east along D 514. As you near the bridge (also new, replacing the 1944 Eiffel bridge in 1971) note a memorial to your left marking the field (LZ Y) where gliders Nos. 95 and 96 came down.

The third glider (No. 94) in this assault force lost its bearings and landed miles to the northeast near Varaville.

There were no defensive positions at the western end of this bridge, but there were machine guns emplacements located on the bank on the eastern side. After landing, Lt. Dennis Fox led his platoon from glider No. 96 in an assault on those emplacements and, aided by a direct hit from a 2-inch mortar, overran them quickly. The sappers discovered that, as was the case at the Pegasus Bridge, there were no demolition charges in place. After being reinforced by Lt. Tod Sweeney's platoon from glider No. 95, the commanders at the Horsa Bridge informed Major Howard of their success, allowing him to broadcast the famous message, "Ham and Jam," to alert senior Airborne commanders that the bridges were in British hands.

Merville Battery

To reach the Merville Battery from Mémorial Pegasus, drive east across the Horsa Bridge on D 514. Just past the bridge, the highway swings north through Sallenelles before swinging east again. Turn right at the traffic light in Merville-Franceville and follow the signs to the Battery, located just off D 223.

According to Allied intelligence estimates, the Merville Battery housed four casemated 150-mm guns sited so they could fire on ships standing off Sword Beach. Eliminating this threat was the task of Lieutenant Colonel Terrance B. H. Otway's 700-man 9th Parachute Battalion. The plan that Otway and his men had been rehearsing for months was daring. Otway's main force would drop some distance from the battery, recover its special equipment — that included bangalore torpedoes, flamethrowers, and anti-tank guns — and then rendezvous just outside the battery's perimeter. This force, divided into eleven teams, would lay the torpedoes under the perimeter wire, mark passages through minefields, and then take up covering positions to await the arrival of two tow-planes with their gliders. On seeing Otway's signal (a star shell fired from a mortar), the gliders were to be cut loose allowing them to land inside the battery perimeter. The 160-man garrison would then be overcome by this combined assault from the air and ground, after which Otway would signal the capture of the battery with red-green-red mortar flares, fired off before 0530, the time HMS *Arethusa* of the Sword Beach bombardment force would take it under fire.

That was the complicated plan that had been rehearsed on a scale mock-up nine times in the month preceding the invasion. Of course on the morning of 6 June, nothing went exactly according to plan. Otway's paras were scattered over a 50-mile corridor; some sticks were never located. He was able to assemble only 150 of his men by the time the attack was to commence. Most of the special equipment, including the mortar signal rounds, carried on two gliders, likewise never arrived. The frustrated men on the ground could only look skyward as the two gliders carrying the assault force circled the low across the casemates and, receiving no signal, came down outside the battery's perimeter. Otway maintained his composure, for no sooner had the gliders arrived and while the defenders were distracted he gave the signal for the attack, shouting: "Get in! Get in!" In short order, the assault troops blew the wire and rushed through the poorly marked minefields. The fight was over in 30 minutes, the casemates breached, and the guns (less formidable Czech 100-mm weapons) disabled with Gammon grenades and other improvised means. With other missions to undertake that day, Otway then withdrew his men almost a mile to the southwest to a Calvary alongside D 223. The assault force had been reduced to 80 combatants.

The entrance to the battery is marked by memorial to the 9 Para Battalion and there is a bust of Col. Otway near the perimeter of the battery where the paras breached the wire. A C-47 aircraft, the "Snafu Special" (recovered from Bosnia-Herzegovina in 2007), and a British field artillery piece are located on the site a short distance from Casemate No. 1. That casemate, renovated in 1982 by British Royal Engineers, now houses a small museum, the Musée de la Batterie. The museum is open daily 15 February through 31 March, 1000-1700; 1 April through 30 September, 0930-1830; and 1 October through 16 November, 1000-1700. Admission charged.

RANVILLE COMMONWEALTH WAR CEMETERY

Before returning to your base of operations, you might consider visiting the Commonwealth Cemetery in Ranville

The importance of Ranville and its suburb, le Bas de Ranville, was that they covered the southern approach to the two Orne bridges. The job of holding that line fell to the 12 Paras who fought off numerous German counterattacks on D-Day and in the days that followed.

The cemetery can be reached from the roundabout just east of the Horsa Bridge by exiting on D 37, which in Ranville becomes the Rue de Stade. From the Rue de Stade turn right onto Sente Moray and then left on the Rue the Rue Airbornes 10. The cemetery entrance, with very limited parking, is on your right. Signs mark the route.

There are 2,235 Commonwealth burials here, along with 330 German and a few of other nationalities. In the nearby churchyard there are 47 Commonwealth burials and one German.

To end your tour and return to Bayeux, drive back across the Orne bridges to the Bénouville junction and turn left onto D 515. Follow D 515 to the Caen ring road (N814), and then swing west until you pick up the N 13-E 3-E 46 to Bayeux.

NIGHT FALLS ON D-DAY

As D-Day ended, senior commanders must have felt some relief that the worst-case scenarios had been averted. None of the landings had been totally successful in achieving their D-Day objectives, but all were ashore with every prospect of remaining there. The airborne assault had not resulted in the unacceptably high casualties that Air Chief Marshal Leigh-Mallory had predicted. The counter-attack of the 21St Panzer Division had been blunted and the wedge it had driven into the gap between the Canadians landing on Juno Beach and the British 3d Division coming ashore on Sword was no longer a threat. And, most importantly, the near-disaster on Omaha Beach had been averted by the courage and desperation of the GIs of the 16th and 116th RLTs, the combat engineers and hundreds of unheralded sailors.

Behind Omaha Beach, GIs held a shallow line only a few hundred yards deep. The Rangers landing on the far right had been unable to hookup with Rudder's men on the Pointe du Hoc, although one platoon had slipped through the German defenses. Most troops landing in the east had done so through exit E-1 where a tank traffic jam of sorts had developed when surviving Shermans of the 741St Tank Battalion clogged the single exit road. Most of the beach exits were still under sporadic artillery and machinegun fire; Exits D-1, D-3 and E-3 remained only partially open. The village of St-Laurent was still in German hands.

Despite the tenuous hold on Omaha, by 1900 both Generals Gerhardt and Huebner had established divisional command posts ashore and later that evening Gen. Gerow landed with his staff to establish the V Corps command post, apply named "Danger Forward." The HQ staff of the 29th Division spent a restless night huddled in a quarry near the Vierville draw, a short distance behind the beach. A mere 100 tons of the projected 2,400 tons of supplies, but nearly 87 percent of the vehicles, had made it ashore. The situation on Omaha Beach remained serious, if no longer critical.

The situation on Utah Beach was less dire. By nightfall, GIs of the 4th Infantry Division had moved three miles inland, making contact with paratroopers of the 101st Airborne. Behind them, support troops moved almost 1,700 tons of supplies and over 1,700 vehicles ashore to support the 21,000 troops that had landed through the beachhead. But, the German 6th Parachute Regiment was not quite willing to relinquish the field, launching a determined counterattack at about 1900 hours. At the same time, American airborne troops were being reinforced by gliders and supply parachute drops that continued well into the night. By the end of D-Day, the German counterattack, which may well have pushed patrols as far as Ste.-Mère-Église, had been snuffed out by a combination of naval gunfire and stiffening resistance in the hedgerows. The tasks left for D-Day + 1 and the days afterward were to link up with the badly scattered 82nd Airborne Division to the west and the Rangers advancing from Omaha Beach to the south.

As was the case on all the landing beaches, the 50th Northumbrian Division failed to reach its D-Day objectives, its penetration inland coming up about 6 km short. Nevertheless, it routed or annihilated the German units opposing it. It had failed to link up the Americans landing on Omaha Beach. There were also serious delays in landing the tanks of the 7th Armoured Division (the "Desert Rats"). Still, some 1,000 tons of supplies were ashore to support the 20,000 "Tommie's" packed inside the bridgehead. During the night of 6-7 June German aircraft flew a number of sorties over Gold Beach, but did little damage. The town of Bayeux was in British hands by noon on June 7. Overall, the Northumbrians suffered 700 casualties on D-Day.

By midnight on D-Day, elements of The Queen's Own Rifles and the North Nova Scotia Highlanders had pushed 11 or 12 km from their landings on the Nan Sectors of June Beach. Their advance had been slowed by resistance at Villons-Buissons and the threat posed by the advance of the 21st Panzer Division in the gap between the Canadians and the British 3rd Division landing over Sword Beach. Gen. Keller ordered both Canadian units to go to ground at Villons-Buissons and the village of Anisy to the east, 6 km short of phase line Oak and the western outskirts of Caen.

It fell to units of the British 3rd Infantry Division landing over Sword Beach to blunt the 21st Panzer Division's drive to the sea between Luc-sur-Mer and Lion-sur-Mer, a thrust that would have isolated Sword Beach and the airborne landings across the Orne River. That German counterattack ended Montgomery's hope of capturing Caen on D-Day. The 3rd Division dug in on a semi-circular line extending roughly from Lion-sur-Mer on the coast to the Orne Canal at Blainville, well short of Caen, knowing full well that the next day would bring another German counterattack.

The real battle for Caen, and for Normandy, was about to begin and would last until the Allied breakout at the end of July.

THE PRICE OF VICTORY

Although universally portrayed as essential and victorious, the D-Day assault on the Normandy coast was not without enormous material and human costs, and it would be an injustice merely to gloss over them.

Bombing, and the fighting that took place within their bounds, heavily damaged a great many Norman cities and towns, most notably Caen and St. Lô. It took at least 20 years to erase the physical scars left by the contending armies, so that today that destruction is virtually invisible to the casual tourist.

Still highly visible after 70 years are the battered reinforced-concrete remnants of the Atlantic wall that scar the coastline and will remain in place into the distant future — a visible reminder of the battles fought here on D-Day.

The human costs of the Battle of Normandy were severe. Some 14,000 civilians in Lower Normandy died as a result of the fighting, mostly from the Allied bombing campaign. Even before the June 6, the implementation of the "Transportation Plan," SHAEF's efforts to isolate the Normandy battlefield by bombing rail yards and bridges, had taken its toll of French civilians — nearly 1,100 casualties in the Sainte-Etienne raid on May 26, 1944 for example. According to Oliver Wieviorka in his recent study, "Normandy: The Landings to the Liberation of Paris" (Cambridge, 2008), between June 1940 and May 1945 there were some 600,000 tons of bombs dropped on France, killing 67,078 people, 35,317 in 1944 alone.

Added to those casualties were the victims of deliberate massacres by members of the German Armed Forces, the most infamous being those at Oradour-sur-Glan, Pommerit-Landy, Plestan and Huelgoat. Some 600 French civilians (including resistance fighters) were summarily executed between June and August 1944.

While there were no reported massacres by Allied troops, there was widespread looting of French property and numerous reported rapes.

The two American Airborne Divisions suffered nearly 5,000 casualties before being withdrawn from combat in early July, while the entire U.S. V Corps had 5,142 men killed, wounded or missing by D-Day+4. Most of those casualties were GIs from the 16th and 116th RCTs who landed in the first assault waves.

The losses among the other Allied forces were fewer on D-Day, but mounted steadily as the campaign continued. The Allied casualties in the Normandy campaign (6 June through mid-August) of 209,672 were a little more than half those of the Wehrmacht, whose total losses amounted to some 393,689 men. It had been a costly victory.

VISITING WORLD WAR II PARIS

You may have some time in Paris to visit WWII sites before, or after, your travel to Normandy. There are numerous WWII memorials and sites scattered around Paris. Many wall plaques commemorating the deaths of Parisians and soldiers killed in the liberation are scattered throughout the city.

Prefecture of Police and Notre Dame Cathedral

Damage is still visible on the façade of the Prefecture of Police from the fighting in August 1944. There is a commemorative plaque on the southeast corner of the building. Across the Rue de la Cité, as you walk toward Notre Dame, notice a number of plaques on the south façade of the Hôtel Dieu commemorating individuals who fell in the fighting.

Hôtel Meurice and the Place de la Concorde

There are plaques on the wall (street level) below the Jeu de Paume Museum commemorating the deaths of soldiers from the French 2nd Armored Division in their attack on Choltitz's headquarters in the Meurice.

The Place itself was the scene of a minor tank battle during which a French Sherman rammed a German Panther during the melee.

Notre-Dame de Paris

Tour Montparnasse

A plaque commemorating Choltitz's surrender at the Gare Montparnasse was relocated to the wall of the C & A Department store occupying part of the base of the 1973 Tour Montparnasse. The old station no longer exists as it was in 1944; its former site now buried beneath the imposing black tower and the new station built behind it.

Two adjacent sites near the Jardin d'Atlantique, a lovely garden on top of the new station, are worth visiting. One is the Musée Jean Moulin and the other is the Mémorial de Maréchal Leclerc de Hauteclocque et de la Libération de Paris. The small Jean Moulin Museum tells the story of the communist resistance leader from Chartres who was exposed and executed by the Nazis in 1943. Marshal Leclerc was, of course, the commander of the 2eme DB during the liberation of Paris. The Mémorial features a film on his career. They are open from 10 a.m. to 6 p.m. and are closed on Monday.

The Catacombs

Resistance forces used the famous Paris ossuary as a headquarters. The catacombs are open most Saturdays after 2 p.m.

Musée de l'Ordre de la Libération

The Museum of the Order of the Liberation is located on the Boulevard Latour-Maubourg in the Hôtel des Invalides. It is devoted to telling the story of the French Resistance during the years of Nazi occupation. Plaques and information cards all in French and are focused on individuals and groups, but if you can translate them they tell an inspiring story. The museum is closed for renovation until June 18, 2015.

Mémorial des Martyrs de la Déportation

This underground memorial to the French Jews deported by the Nazis is located on the eastern most tip Île de la Cité, east of Notre Dame Cathedral. The 200,000 crystals illuminating the crypt serve to remind us of the deportees.

Suresnes American Military Cemetery and Mont Valerien Memorial

The cemetery lies outside the city of Paris per se and can most easily be reached by taking one of the commuter trains that leaves the Gare St.-Lazare every twenty minutes. Suresnes is located directly across the Seine from the Bois de Boulogne. After a short ride the cemetery is about a ten-minute walk up Mont Valerien.

The 7.5-acre World War I cemetery holds the graves of 1,541 doughboys and 24 unknown GIs of World War II. Bronze tablets in the chapel bear the names of 974 soldiers, sailors and airmen of World War I. The two new loggias are dedicated to the dead of both wars. The cemetery is open from 0900-1700 except for Christmas and New Year's Day

In addition to the American cemetery, Mont Valerien is the site of the French "Memorial to Fighting France." The German occupying force executed some 4,500 members of the French resistance on the slopes of this hill from 1940 to 1944.

Musée de l'Armée:

The Army Museum at Les Invalides, founded in 1905 when the Artillery Museum merged with the Army History Museum, has been upgraded over the years. Currently, it tells the story of French military power from medieval times through World War II. It holds an extensive collection of French, British, German and American artifacts related to the Normandy invasion.

The museum is one of the largest of its kind in the world. A visit here is a must stop prior to, or even after, your trip to the battlefields of Normandy.

The Army Museum is open every day, except Christmas and New Year's Day, from 1 April to 31 October, 1000-1800. Winter hours are 1 November to 31 March: Monday to Sunday, 1000 – 1700. Go to the museum's website below for the most current information about operating times and admission cost.

The Museum ticket includes admission to:

- Army Museum's permanent collections

- The Dome Church and tomb of Napoleon I

- Charles de Gaulle Monument

- Museum of Relief Maps

- Museum of the Order of the Liberation (closed for renovation until June 18, 2015)

If you are staying in Paris, a worthwhile and money saving item, the Paris Museum Pass, offers the chance to go to the front of the line at more than 60 museums. You can buy the pass at many hotels—and at the Army Museum. For more information, go to: www.parismuseumpass.com.

The Army Museum also offers a reasonably priced (for Paris) cafeteria with hot dishes and salads ranging from 5-10 euros. Sandwiches are 4-6.50 euros.

The museum has a fine book and gift shop, which is located at the ticket desk on the Place Vauban side of the large complex. The gift shop boasts more than 2,000 items that includes military guides, history books, postcards and other collectables.

For more Army Museum information, go to: http://www.musee-armee.fr/en/english-version.html.

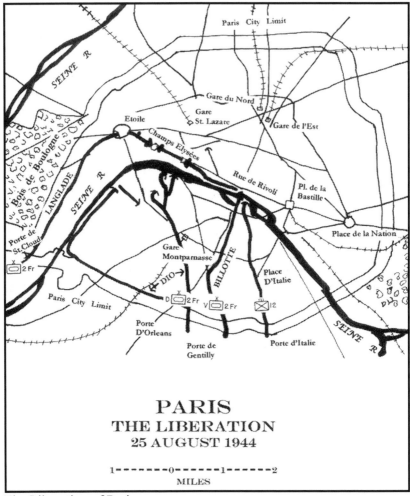

PARIS
THE LIBERATION
25 AUGUST 1944

The Liberation of Paris

Eating and Sleeping in Paris

It is a little presumptuous for us to make recommendations concerning hotels and restaurants in Paris. There is no way that we can do anything other than scratch the surface. We really recommend that you acquire a standard guide to Paris that you have confidence in and ransack it for ideas and suggestions. Meanwhile, here are a few of our own:

Be prepared for sticker-shock despite the dollar's recent rise against the euro because, after all, this is Paris. Eat your big meal of the day at lunch. Lunch menus tend to be less expensive. Eat inside. You will get charged more sitting at those street-side tables.

Many of the smaller ethnic restaurants provide a good value for the euro, especially the North African, Vietnamese, Chinese, and Greek ones. You should also check some of the web sites that rate restaurants, e.g., TripAdvisor for their consumer driven ratings.

Watch your handbags and camera cases at all times. They have a habit of walking off when not minded. Be extra careful in obvious tourist traps. Don't over tip. The service charge is almost always included, but leaving a little extra is always acceptable.

If you can, stay out of hotels that cater to youth groups. You need your sleep.

Don't go below a two star hotel. Three stars will provide you with a dining room and some other amenities.

Paris Restaurants:

Here are a few suggestions for restaurants we can recommend. These tend to be expensive, but far from the most expensive.

Le Petit Zinc – for seafood. 11 rue St. Benoît in the Latin Quarter. Tel. 01-42-61-20-60.

Le Procope – for Latin Quarter atmosphere. Some dining establishment by this name has been open in Paris since the Enlightenment. Sometimes called the oldest coffee shop in the world. 13 rue de l'Ancienne-Comédie. Tel. 01-40-46-79-00.

Le Vaudeville – a classic art deco brassiere across from the Bourse. 29 rue Vivienne. Tel. 01-40-20-04-62.

Restaurant Marrakech – an over the top Moroccan establishment in walking distance from the Arc de Triomphe. 12 rue d'Armaillé. Tel. 01-43-80-26-65.

L'Alcazar – a very chic establishment on the left bank. 62 rue Mazarine. Tel. 01-53-10-19-99.

Les Deux Magots – a Paris landmark. Order the cheapest glass of wine you can (it will be expensive) and people watch away the afternoon. Nurse that wine! 6 Place St.-Germain-des-Prés. Tel. 01-45-48-55-25.

Brasserie Flo – this is another classic brasserie now part of a restaurant group. 7 cour des Petites Écuries. Tel. 01-47-70-13-59.

La Caleche – fixed menus at a reasonable price (if there is such a thing in Paris). 8 Rue de Lille. Tel. 01-42-60-24-76.

La Taverne du Sergent Recruiter – in the past, a military recruiter used to get young men drunk to induce them to enlist in the army here. It's an all-you-can eat joint. Many tourists, but great for families. Ile St. Louis. Tel. 01-43-54-75-42.

Roger la Grenouille – since 1930, this Paris cafe has served such celebrities as Humphrey Bogart, Rita Hayworth, Gen. Leclerc, Gen. George Marshall and others. 28 Rue des Grands-Augustins. Tel. 01-56-24-24-34.

Paris Hotels:

Here you are pretty much on your own. Check the Trip Advisor website for recent guest evaluations.

Mercure Hotels (Tel. 01-53-46-50-50; mercure.com) – The Mercure Hotel chain operates 38 Paris hotels in various price ranges. Consult their website for locations and prices.

If you want to stay in a smaller hotel, we can recommend:

Hôtel des Deux Acacias – 28 rue de l'Arc de Triomphe (Tel. 01-43-80-01-85) very near the Arc de Triomphe.

Hôtel Le Madison – 143 Boulevard St. Germain (Tel. 01-40-51-60-00) is also a nice choice and centrally located on the left bank.

Both of the above hotels have web sites where you can glean more information and make reservations.

Two three-star Left Bank hotels include:

Hotel Bersoly's Saint Germain is a small hotel that dates from the 17th Century, 28 Rue de Lille (Tel. 01-42-60-73-79), hotelbersolys@wanadoo.fr

Hotel Lenox Saint Germain – 9 Rue de L'universite, another boutique hotel with a good continental breakfast, 01-42-96-10-95, hotel@lenoxsaintgermain.com.

APPENDIX

THE LEADERS
Allied Expeditionary Force High Command, 1944

General Dwight D. Eisenhower
Supreme Commander, Allied Expeditionary Force

Air Chief Marshal Sir Arthur Tedder
Deputy Supreme Commander

Admiral Sir Bertram Ramsey
C-in-C Allied Naval Forces

Air Chief Marshal Sir Trafford Leigh-Mallory
C-in-C Allied Air Forces

General Sir Bernard L. Montgomery
Commander, 21st Army Group

Lt. General Omar N. Bradley
Commander, First U. S. Army

Lt. General Sir Miles Dempsey
Commander, Second Army (British and Canadian)

German High Command in Normandy, 1944

Generalfeldmarschall Gerd von Rundstedt
Oberfelshaber West (OB West)

Generalfeldmarschall Erwin Rommel
Armeegruppe B

Generalfeldmarschall Hugo Sperrle
Luftflotte 3

Admiral Theodore Kranke
Marinegruppenkommando West

Generaloberst Friedrich Dollmann
7. Armee

General der Panzertruppe Geyr von Schweppenburg
Panzergruppe West

D-DAY MILITARY MUSEUMS

There are other military museums in Normandy besides those included in this section. With the exception of Mémorial du Caen, the following list includes the major museums nearest the Allied landing beaches and drop-zones. See the individual museum's website for current admission charges and opening times.

Arromanches-les-Bain

The **Musée du Debarquement**, one of the more interesting of the D-Day museums, is open daily May through August from 0900 to 1900. Opening times vary for the remainder of the year. Web: www.musee-arromanches.fr for updated details. Admission charged.

Bayeux

The **Musée-Mémorial de la Bataille de Normandy** displays an impressive number of military artifacts and uniformed mannequins that pay tribute to the multitude of military units that fought here during the summer of 1944. Phone: +33(0)2.31.51.46.90; Fax: +33(0)2.31.51.46.91; Web: www.mairie-bayeux.fr. Open 1000-1230 and 1400-1800 daily from October 1 to April 30; 0930-1830 from May 1 to September 30. Closed January 1 to February 15. Admission charged.

Caen

Memorial du Caen (Esplanade Général Eisenhower), located off the N 13 périphérique (N 814) that circles Caen to the north, is the most impressive military museums in Normandy and one of the best in the world. (Exit the périphérique at Sortie 7, and then pass through two roundabouts to the museum. Signs mark the turnoff from all directions.) Opened in September 1986, Memorial aims "to set the operations of 6 June and the Battle of Normandy into the context of the Second World War by recalling the conflict's distant origins and its many consequences." These goals are achieved at the highest level through displays, A-V presentations, photographs, and artifacts. The museum encompasses Memorial Gardens, three restaurants, a bookstore/souvenir shop and an extensive library. The museum also conducts tours of the landing beaches. You should not miss Memorial during your stay in Normandy. Phone: +33(0)2.31.06.06.44; Fax: +33(0)2.31.06.01.66; email: resa@memorial-caen.fr; Web: www.memorial-caen.fr. Open daily February 6 to November 10, 0900-1900; November 12 to December 31, 0930 – 1800 daily, except for Mondays (excluding December 23 and 30 2013); closed Christmas day and January 6 - 28. Admission charged. See the museum's online schedule for individual, group and combination (with Arromanches 360) admissions.

An exhibit in Memorial du Caen

Carentan

The Normandy Tank Museum and A-10 Airfield, opened on June 1, 2013, houses the WWII collection of Patrick Nerrant and his sons, Stéphane and Olivier. Their collection is comprised of a number of fully restored American military vehicles and aircraft, including several tanks, a M 7 Priest (motorized 105-mm howitzer), motorcycles and a L4H Grasshopper (Piper Cub) in its D-Day markings. Touts itself as the largest museum in Normandy with 10,170-square-feet of exhibition halls exhibiting more than 40 military vehicles and 11,000 artifacts from the war on 10 acres. The museum is situated on a 1944 airstrip. Tank rides and demonstrations are featured. The museum, located off the old N 13 just east of Carentan, can be reached by exiting the "new" N 13-E 3-E 46 *autoroute* at the Carentan interchange. Enter the north roundabout to double back on the "old" N 13 (now D 974, the Ave. du Cotentin) for 1 km, just past the village of La Fourchette. Ph: +33(0)2.33.44.39.45; contact@Normandy-tank-museum.fr; www.normandy-tank-museum.fr. Open daily from April 1 to October 31, 0900-1800; November 1 to March 31, 1000-1700; closed from December 31 to January 31. Admission charged.

Dead Man's Corner Museum (Centre Historique des Parachutistes du Jour-J) and The Airborne Memorial Wall This gem of a museum is located in a small house at the junction of D 913 and D 974 between St-Côme-du-Mont and Carentan. The building was used as a German command post on D-Day. Today, the museum exhibits a fascinating collection of mementos, uniformed mannequins and equipment used by the airborne forces, American and German, that fought here. The name "Dead Man's Corner" was given to the intersection by men of the 101st AD because of a dead tank crewman hanging from an exit hatch of his disabled Stuart light tank at the intersection. Phone: +33(0)2.33.42.00.42; airborne.carentan@gmail.com. Open daily from 0900-1800 except Sundays, October 1, April 30, December 24 and 25 and January 1. Admission charged.

The "Airborne Memorial Wall" is a small commemorative wall, located behind the museum, bearing plaques honoring individuals from the airborne units that fought here. Among the men so honored to date are Richard Winters, Bill Guarnere and Darrell C. "Shifty" Powers, all members of Easy Company, 506th PI, 101st AD, Stephen E. Ambrose's "Band of Brothers."

Dead Man's Corner Museum was the scene of heavy fighting

The Cole Bayonet Charge Memorial This new memorial stele is located just off D 974 about a kilometer southeast of the Dead Man's Corner Museum. It is very near bridge #4 over the Douve River where LTC Robert G. Cole led his 3rd Battalion, 502nd PR in its famous bayonet charge on June 11, 1944. Military personnel, including a contingent from the 101st AD, and civilian dignitaries dedicated the memorial in an impressive ceremony on June 4, 2014.

A four-foot square, flat, granite slab bearing a lithograph depicting Cole, 1SGT Ken Sprechier and Pvts. Allen Emory and Edward Sower adorns the base of the stele. All four men were cited for their bravery during the attack, with Cole receiving the Medal of Honor posthumously. In September, a German sniper near the Dutch town of Best killed Cole during the opening days of Operation Market-Garden, just before the Medal of Honor could be officially awarded. Another memorial to Col. Cole stands near Best.

Cherbourg

The Musée de la Libération is located in the Fort du Roule outside the city. Exhibits trace the history of Cherbourg during the war, including D-Day and its subsequent liberation by the U.S. Army. Open from May to September, Tuesday-Saturday, 1000-1200, 1400-1800; October–April, Wednesday-Sunday 1400-1800. Closed on public holidays. Admission free.

Colleville-sur-Mer

Big Red One Assault Museum. This small museum is dedicated to retelling the story of the men of the 1st United States Infantry Division, whose 16th Infantry Regiment spearheaded the assault on Omaha Beach on D-Day. The museum's displays are derived from the collection of the owner and curator, Pierre-Louis Gosselin, and consist of personal artifacts and mementos relating to the Big Red One's experience in Normandy. It is located at Hameau-du-Bray, just west of Colleville-sur-Mer, off D 514. Open from January 1 to November 30 with variable hours depending on the time of year. For more information regarding opening and closing times see the Normandy tourism website: www.normandy-tourism.org. Phone: +33(0)2.31.21.53.81; Email: bigredoneassaultmuseum@gmail.com. Admission charged.

The **Overlord Museum** is housed in a new, modernistic building just off the D 514 roundabout that also takes you into the Normandy American Military Cemetery. It's impossible to miss because of its size, signage and the Sherman tank that marks the entrance road. The museum displays the personal collection of the late Michel Leloup, which includes 35 military vehicles and guns, a Bailey bridge, documents and posters relating the Allied invasion. Inside are scenic recreations of many of the important engagements that make up the Battle of Normandy that utilize models and mannequins. Open daily with variable times from March 1 to late December. Closed December 23 to 26 & 31 and all of January and February. For further information regarding opening and closing times see the museum website. Phone: +33 (0)2.31.22.00.55; Fax: +33(0)2.31.22.13.15; Web: www.overlordmuseum.com/en/; Email: contact@overlordmuseum.com. Admission charged.

Courseulles-sur-Mer

Juno Beach Centre. This impressive new museum features exhibits concerning Canadian participation on all fronts during WWII as well as with contemporary Canadian society. The Centre also provides tours of the landing beaches. Open daily from February 1 to December 31 with variable times. Closed January. For further information regarding opening and closing times see the Centre's website. Phone: +33 (0)2.31.37.32.17; Fax: +33(0)2.31.37.83.69; Website: www.junebeach.org; Email: contact@junobeach.org.

Grandcamp-Maisy.

The Musée des Rangers (30 Quai Crampon) was opened in this fishing village in 1990. Using storyboards, photographs and equipment, this small museum retells the story of Lt. Col. James Earl Rudder's 2d Ranger Battalion from its creation to its D-Day assault on the Pointe du Hoc. The 18-minute A-V presentation running on the second floor relies heavily on clips from the film *The Longest Day*, and from Walter Cronkite's 1964 battlefield tour with Gen. Dwight D. Eisenhower. Phone: +33(0)2.31.22.64.34. Open: February 15 – April 30, Tuesday — Sunday, 1300-1800, closed Mondays. Open: May 1 – October 31, Wednesday – Sunday, 1000-1300 and 1430-1830 and Tuesday afternoons,1330-1830, closed Monday and Tuesday mornings. Closed: November 1 – February 14. Admission charged.

Merville

Musée de la Batterie. This recently renovated museum is open daily from February 15 through March 15, 1000-1700, from April 1 through September 30, 0930-1830 and October 1 through November 16, 1000-1700. Admission charged.

Ouistreham-River Bella

Musée du Commando No. 4. This small museum, located right behind the rebuilt casino, is dedicated to retelling the story of the No. 4 Commando's landing on Sword Beach. Open every day from mid-March to late October, 1030-1300 and 1330-1830. Ph: +33(0)2.31.98.83.10. Email: info@musee-4commando.org. Web: www.musee-4commando.org. Admission charged.

Musée le Mur de l'Atlantique. This museum occupies all six floors of a fully restored German artillery command post. Open every day 1000-1800, 1 February to 31 December; 0900-1900, 1 April to 30 September. Phone:

+33(0)2.31.97.28.69; Fax: +33(0)2.31.96.66.05. Email: bunkermusee@aol.com. Admission charged.

Port-en-Bessin

Musée des Epaves sous-marines du Débarquement displays the efforts of almost thirty years work in recovering personal items, equipment from the sea floor that was lost during the D-Day invasion. Fascinating stuff. Ph: +33(0)2.31.21.17.06. Open from June 1 to September 30 and holidays in May. Admission charged.

St. Laurent-sur-Mer

The Musée Mémorial d'Omaha Beach is a small museum located on the Rue de la Mer, a short distance inland from the beach, contains artifacts and displays related to the landings. Ph: +33(0)2.31.21.97.44; FX: +33(0)2.31.92.72.80. Website: www.musee-memorial-omaha.com. Open from February 15 to March 15, 100-1230 and 1430 to 1800; March 16 to May 15, 0930-1830; May 16 to September 15, 0930 to 1900 (in July and August open 0930 to 1930); September 16 to November 15, 0930 to 1830. The last admission is an hour before closing time. Admission charged.

Ste-Marie-du-Mont

The Musée du Débarquement Utah Beach was the brainchild of Michael de Vallavieille, mayor of Sainte-Marie-du-Mont in 1962, the year the museum opened. In its first iteration the museum occupied the German strongpoint WN-5 in front of which the 8th Infantry mistakenly came ashore on D-Day. Today, a vastly expanded and rebuilt museum occupies the same site, surrounded by numerous memorials and monuments. The new museum houses a rich collection of military equipment, arms, photographs and other artifacts of the landing including a Martin B-26G Marauder (Dinah Might) in its D-Day markings. Ph: +33(0)2.33.71.53.35; Fax: +33(0)2.33.71.92.36. Web: www.utah-beach.com. Open every day in June, July and August 0930-1900; October through May, 1000-1800. Closed in January. Admission charged.

Ste.-Mère-Église

The **Musée Airborne** contains exhibits, artifacts, various weapons and mementos of the airborne landings in and around the town in the early hours of D-Day. In 1964, Lt. Gen. James Gavin, assistant commander of the 82d Airborne Division on D-Day, opened the museum that is covered with a roof designed like a fluted parachute canopy. The museum's exit is through the body of a Waco glider. Don't skip the Annex that houses one of the C-47s, "Argonia," of the 439th Troop Carrier Group that actually flew missions on D-Day. A well-preserved M-4A1E8 "Easy Eight" Sherman tank and an American 90-mm anti-aircraft gun are displayed on the museum grounds. Open every day February 1 to March 31, 1000-1700; April 1 to September 30, 0900-1845; October 1 to December 30, 1000-1700. Closed December 24, 25, 31 and the month of January. The new exhibit hall, named Operation Neptune, featuring the Argonia and the interactive experience of a squad of paratroopers from the 82nd Airborne Division as it prepares to jump into Normandy--was the first major addition to the museum since 1984. Web: www.airborne-museum.org; Phone: +33(0)2. 33.41.41.35 ; Fax: +33(0)2.33.41.78.87.

Musée Omaha at Vierville-sur-Mer

Ver-sur-Mer

Musée America Gold Beach. This hybrid museum is dedicated to retelling both the story of the assault on Gold Beach and the 1927 trans-Atlantic flight of Adm. Richard Byrd, whose airplane, "America," crash landed off the Ver-sur-Mer beach. Open daily in July and August from 1030 to 1730. The times are the same in April, May, June, September and October, but the museum is closed on Tuesdays. It is closed from November through March, except by prior arrangement. Telephone: +33(0)2.31.22.58.58; Fax: +33(0)2.31.21.09.12; www.goldbeachmusee.org.uk.

Vierville-sur-Mer

Vierville is home to the **Musée D Day Omaha**, housed in what looks to be an old hangar on the Route de Grandcamp. The museum displays exhibits featuring documents, photographs and equipment relating to the landings on Omaha Beach. Phone/Fax: +33(0)2.31.21.71.80; Web: www.vierville-sur-mer.com. Open April to November; June through September, 0930-1930 daily. No admission information given.

RESOURCES FOR D-DAY TRAVELERS

Travelling to Normandy takes methodical planning. During summer months, particularly around June 6, many hotels rooms are filled up near the beach, official ceremonies restricted due to security, as many heads of state will attend—and traffic will be heavy. Always go to our Facebook page and website to find up-to-date D-Day events, notifications and other vital information.

The information below will give you a starting point, but remember, activities change constantly, so don't be caught unaware on the way to the beaches!

A good starting point is our website. For updated information, go to www.dday70th.com. Updates to this guidebook, events, good restaurants, drink and sleep are featured. In addition, share your thoughts about D-Day with other readers and make suggestions on places to see.

TripAdvisor, www.tripadvisor.com, is always a great source of available hotel and restaurant information, with the requisite ratings of many hotels. In addition, cheap lodging can be found in many apartments via Airbnb, www.airbnb.com

WHAT IF YOU CAN'T MAKE IT TO NORMANDY THIS SUMMER?

Well, there are (No?) alternative sites that you might consider visiting that are closer to home. Both provide an excellent way to commemorate D-Day that are informative and can be driven to.

The National D-Day Memorial:
The memorial is located outside the southwest Virginia town of Bedford for a reason. One of the regiments chosen to spearhead the attack on Omaha Beach was the 116th IR of the 29th U.S. Infantry Division, a unit created from the National Guards of Virginia, Maryland, Pennsylvania and District of Columbia. Inducted into federal service on February 3, 1941, the division was extensively trained in the United States before being deployed to England in October 1942. After what seemed like an interminable wait, Overlord planners chose the untested 116th Infantry to represent the National Guard in the first waves at Omaha Beach.

Company A, 1st Battalion, 116th IR, now attached to the 1st Infantry Division for the assault, listed 34 young men from Bedford (pop. 3,200) in its ranks. These GIs became famous after D-Day as the Bedford Boys because 19 of them gave their lives on Omaha Beach; four other Bedford Boys were killed later in the battle, including two more from other companies. (For a closer look at the fate of Company A, see our account under "Omaha Beach.") The last of the Bedford Boys, Lt. Ray Nance died in April 2009 at the age of 94.

The 88-acre Memorial, dedicated in 2001 by then President George W. Bush, contains a wealth of exhibits pertaining to D-Day, including a mock-up of a small section of Omaha Beach and numerous commemorative statues and memorials. Throughout the year the Memorial staff conducts programs related to D-Day; tours of the Memorial are sometimes conducted by D-Day veterans and will be as long as they are with us.

More detailed information is found on the Memorial's excellent web site, www.dday.org. Phone: 1-800-351-DDAY or 540-556-3329; email: dday@dday.org.

Bedford is located between Roanoke and Lynchburg off U.S. highway 221/460.

The National WWII Museum:
Largely the inspiration of historian Stephen E. Ambrose, then a professor at The University of New Orleans, this museum opened on June 6, 2000 as The National D-Day Museum. A few years later, Congress renamed it The National WWII Museum to better reflect its growth and the enlarged scope of its mission.

Located in central New Orleans, the museum contains exhibits, documents and artifacts relating to all aspects of WWII. Possibly the crowning presentation is the film, "Beyond All Boundaries," an epic, visual history of the war produced by Tom Hanks and shown on an enormous surround screen in the Solomon Victory Theater. Final Mission: The USS *Tang* Experience takes visitors on the *Tang*'s fifth and final combat patrol so they may experience life on an American submarine.

For additional information see the museum's web site, www.nationalww2museum.org or call 504-528-1944. Basic adult admission to the museum is $22 with additional charges for the special shows.

A visit to either of these sites would be a fine way to celebrate the courage of American service men and women on the 70th anniversary of D-Day and to visit some interesting sections of the country as well. Both have a full program of special events scheduled. We don't that you will be disappointed with either the Memorial or the Museum or, for that matter, any of the many other military museums scattered around the nation.

MOVIE REVIEWS

While not essential to understanding the Normandy battlefield, the educational value of these two films to the traveler is high. And, it's always fun to confront the Hollywood take on WWII. These two famous films about D-Day should help you better appreciate the battle as it has been presented to the American public through the camera lens.

The Longest Day (1962)
Saving Private Ryan (1998)

One can't help but wonder if Darryl F Zanuck knew what he was getting into when he purchased the film rights to Cornelius Ryan's "The Longest Day" for a reputed $175,000. The task that he set for himself and his three directors, Ken Annakin, Andrew Marton and Bernhard Wicki were formidable. A short 18 years after the event, Zanuck discovered that the weapons and equipment used, and the uniforms worn by the combatants in 1944 were passing rapidly from the scene. Authentic weapons in working order were hard enough to find, but ammunition, that was another thing entirely. Some had to be remanufactured. New uniforms had to be sewn in Paris; German cigarette packages and candy wrappers copied from museum originals. Zanuck even had trouble finding a 48-star American flag. Frustrated, he is reported to have said that Ike had the men and material to stage D-Day, but that he had neither!

His problems didn't end there. How do you stage a massive airborne drop such as occurred in Normandy? Why, you film a British army practice drop in Cyprus. In the days before computer generated animation, how do you stage an amphibious landing with real ships and landing craft? Why, you engage the help of the U.S. 6th Fleet and film a practice landing with 1,600 Marines on the deserted beaches of Corsica. Fortunately, there were lots of American LCVPs (Higgins boats) and DUKWs still around in the early 60s. Unfortunately, British troops had to be filmed landing from LCVPs as well; the 6th Fleet must have been a little short of LCAs.

Oily black smoke from burning vehicles on the beach could be faked by burning some of production's stockpile of 25,000 used car tires. But, the two Spitfires that strafe a German column and wreck a perfectly lovely VW Type 82 Kübelwagen were the real thing, reclaimed from the Belgian air force and flown for the film by Pierre Laureys, a Free French ace during the war. At one point, a pundit quipped that Zanuck's outfit was the world's ninth ranked military power.

The real Ste.-Mère-Église was used to film the disastrous night drop, and a section of coastline not far from the Pointe du Hoc was used to stage the Ranger assault. Much of the rest could be done with on sets with smoke and mirrors.

Casting was apparently less of a problem. Every notable male actor in Hollywood, and some who weren't so notable, seems to have scrounged a part. What other movie can you name casts Rod Steiger, Richard Burton and Sean Connery in bit parts and then throws in John Wayne, Henry Fonda, Robert Mitchum in major roles. And the list goes on for a total of over 40 names listed in the credits. Many of the lesser-known actors playing Germans have more speaking lines (in German no less, with subtitles) than do the Americans. And thanks to Wicki's direction, they appear in some of the more realistic scenes. Eisenhower, Bradley and Montgomery hardly make a show. But then, that's the way Ryan wrote the book and the screenplay. The film is one of the first I can remember to involve so many characters in sequential scenes with abrupt cuts between them. Sometimes the pace is dizzying, but somehow the direction and audience familiarity with many of the actors manage to carry the plot forward. And, does it really matter whether or not you can remember exactly who Gen. Erich Marcks was?

The main objection that I have to the film is the woodenness of the dialog. Zanuck tried his hand at rewriting Ryan's efforts, then called in the World War II novelist, James Jones. Jones livened things up, but his script ran afoul of the censors at the Production Code Office. Out went euphemisms such as "crap," "mother lover," muck it," and all the rest. Realism suffers.

Without employing a background narrator, it fell to the principal characters to fill in the strategic and tactical situations by carefully explaining the details to their staffs (who had probably just briefed them) or to others who were unfortunate enough to be standing near by. Watching the film is at times like sitting through a 180-minute history lecture, sometimes enlightening, but awfully tedious.

Then there is the matter of violence. War is violent; a frontal assault on a fortified beach is really violent. "The Longest Day" doesn't shirk violence, but it's the '50s type. Soldiers are shot, clutch their chests and fall to the ground. It's not at all gory, but that may be in part because it was filmed in black and white (although a colorized, digital version is available on DVD for the non-purist).

Contrast Zanuck's approach to war with Steven Spielberg's opening scene in "Saving Private Ryan." There is no long lead-in to set the stage for the action as there is in "The Longest Day." You are not even told where you are. You see a sun-drenched American flag flapping lazily in the breeze. You see an old man with his family walking along a path overlooking the sea. He is crying. Only when he turns onto a grassy sward and rows of marble crosses and stars appear do you realize that he is in a military cemetery. He falls to his knees before a cross and the camera zooms in on his eyes. Then you are in an LCVP with Capt. John H. Miller (Tom Hanks) and 29 other Rangers headed for some God forsaken beach. (Spielberg assumes that you don't need a history lesson, but he does err in leading the viewer to assume that the 2nd Ranger Battalion previously had served in the

Mediterranean theater.) Miller's hand shivers as he drinks from his canteen; he barks instructions to his men. Then the ramp drops and the world as these men knew it ends. The next 22 minutes are among the most traumatizing ever put on film. There is no way to describe it except to say that there is blood and dismemberment and heroism. And, there is also coolness under fire and true grit. You don't so much see it as you experience it.

It's too bad that the film slides downhill from there--in the sense that it reverts to a more ordinary World War II combat film, but one with more than a few expletives. Once again you have a disparate group of American GIs trying to make the best of a bad situation. You have seen them before in "Battleground," "The Sands of Iwo Jima" and even more recently in "A Midnight Clear." But it doesn't slide very far, because soon you find yourself empathizing with Miller and his squad as they search for the mythical Private James Ryan (Matt Damon), the last of four sons of an Iowa farm mother. (The story is based on the real life Niland brothers from Buffalo, NY, three of whom were in Normandy. One brother, Fritz, was withdrawn from combat when it was thought that all three of his brothers had been killed.)

"Saving Private Ryan" is redeemed by the final scenes depicting the inevitable German counterattack at a bridge on the Merderet River, redeemed at the moment you realize there is not going to be a short-term happy outcome. You can see it in the men's faces and hear it in Edith Piaf's voice playing over an ancient phonograph. Yes, they have saved Private Ryan, but you have a gut feeling that the price is going to be very high.

Whether or not there is redemption in screenwriter Robert Rodat's final maudlin scene in the St. Laurent cemetery, I'll let you decide.

Between them, these films won seven Academy Awards – special effects and cinematography for "The Longest Day," and best director, editing, cinematography, sound and sound effects editing for "Saving Private Ryan" – all well deserved. There were numerous other awards as well.

"Saving Private Ryan" engendered further controversy in November 2004 when, in deference to the objections raised by the American Family Association, 68 affiliates of the ABC network cancelled a Veterans Day showing. The reasons given were the expletives used and the "graphic violence" in the battle scenes. The 68 affiliates were apparently afraid of being fined by the FCC if they went ahead with the broadcast; many other affiliates ran the film with the usual commercial breaks.

SUGGESTED READING

Here are a small group of very good books that we have culled from the vast number published about D-Day and the Battle of Normandy. They are all currently available through Amazon.com and other outlets.

HISTORIES

Ambrose, Stephen E. *D-Day, June 6, 1944: The Climatic Battle of World War II* (1994).
- *Pegasus Bridge: June 6, 1944* (1985).
- *Band of Brothers: E Company, 506th Regiment, 101st Airborne from Normandy to Hitler's Eagle Nest* (1992).

Beevor, Anthony. *D-Day: The Battle for Normandy* (2003).

D'Este, Carlo. *Decision in Normandy* (1983).

Falconer, Jonathan. *D-Day, 'Neptune,' 'Overlord' and the Battle of Normandy: Operations Manual* (2013).

Hastings, Max. *Overlord: Day-Day and the Battle for Normandy* (1984).

Isby, David C. *Fighting the Invasion: The German Army at D-Day* (2000)

Keegan, John. *Six Armies in Normandy* (1982).

Lewis, Adrian R. *Omaha Beach: A Flawed Victory* (2001).

Macintyre, Ben. *Double Cross: The True Story of the D-Day Spies* (2012).

Ryan, Cornelius. *The Longest Day, June 6, 1944* (1959).

Wieviorka, Oliver. *Normandy: The Landings to the Liberation of Paris* (2008).

MEMOIRS

Bradley, Omar N. *A General's Life; An Autobiography* (1984).

Burgette, Donald R. *Currahee!* (1967).

Cawthon, Charles R. *Other Clay. A Remembrance of World War II Infantry* (1990).

Eisenhower, Dwight D. *Crusade in Europe* (1948).

Lovat, Lord. *March Past* (1978).

Montgomery, Bernard L. *The Memoirs of Field-Marshal the Viscount Montgomery of Alamein, KG* (1958).

GUIDES

Holt, Tonie and Valmaie. *Major and Mrs. Holt's Definitive Battlefield Guide to the D-Day Normandy Landings, 6th Ed.* (2012).

Holt, Tonie and Valmaie. *Major and Mrs. Holt's Pocket Battlefield Guide to Normandy* (2009, 2012).

Eleven years ago Sutton Publishing came out with a series of 188-page hardback guides to the Battle of Normandy under the general editorship of Simon Trew. Together they are called the "Battle Zone Normandy" Series. All are well researched and contain a wealth of material on the landings and the memorials that commemorate them. The volumes most pertinent to the landing beaches themselves are:

Badsey, Stephen and Tim Bean. *Omaha Beach* (2004).

Badsey, Stephen. *Utah Beach* (2004)

Clark, Lloyd. *Orne Bridgehead* (2004).

Ford, Ken. *Sword Beach* (2004).

Ford, Ken. *Juno Beach* (2004).

Trew, Simon. *Gold Beach* (2004).

ABOUT THE AUTHORS

Stephen T. Powers

Professor Stephen T. Powers is the author of *The March to Victory, A Guide to World War II Battles and Battlefields from London to the Rhine*. A U.S. Naval Academy graduate, Powers was a history professor at the University of Northern Colorado for more than 30 years.

Kevin Dennehy

Kevin Dennehy has been a journalist for more than 28 years, writing for daily newspapers and magazines. A retired Army National Guard colonel, Dennehy is a combat veteran of Afghanistan and Iraq.

NOTES

Made in the USA
San Bernardino, CA
08 June 2017